# The Ultimate

# FRUGAL
# LIVING

# The Ultimate Guide to

# FRUGAL LIVING

## Save Money, Plan Ahead, Pay Off Debt & Live Well

# DAISY LUTHER

### author of *Be Ready for Anything*

Racehorse Publishing

Racehorse Publishing books may be purchased in bulk at special discounts for sales promotion, corporate gifts, fund-raising, or educational purposes. Special editions can also be created to specifications. For details, contact the Special Sales Department, Skyhorse Publishing, 307 West 36th Street, 11th Floor, New York, NY 10018 or info@skyhorsepublishing.com.

Racehorse Publishing™ is a pending trademark of Skyhorse Publishing, Inc.®, a Delaware corporation.

Visit our website at www.skyhorsepublishing.com.

10 9 8 7 6 5 4

Library of Congress Cataloging-in-Publication Data is available on file.

Cover design by Daniel Brount
Cover illustration by gettyimages

Print ISBN: 978-1-63158-600-2
Ebook ISBN: 978-1-63158-601-9

Printed in China

This book is dedicated to Amy Dacyczyn. She doesn't know me or anything. I'm just a fangirl. Her warmth, advice, adorable illustrations, and compassion helped me through more than one difficult time. Her work completely changed the course of my life and helped me find hope when I felt the most hopeless. *The Tightwad Gazette* put me on a path that helped me survive poverty, loss, single motherhood, and the launch of a dream, all with my head held high. If any of you know Amy, please tell her I said "thank you" from the bottom of my heart.

# Table of Contents

# *Introduction*

It's tough to make ends meet these days, and I know it's not just me. Personal financial problems seem to be an epidemic lately. Gone are the days when a person works at the same stable job until they get handed a nice watch at their retirement party. Gone are the days when medical care and insurance were affordable. Gone are the days when you could fill a grocery cart with cheap basics for less than $50 per week. Sometimes you're winning financially, and sometimes you're losing. Throughout my adult life, I have learned that financial stability is an illusion for most of us. I've worked hard and made some pretty decent money. I've scrimped and gotten by on an astonishingly small amount of money. And through it all, the lesson that was repeated over and over is that *it can all change in the blink of an eye.*

One day you have a great job. The next day, the business for which you work folds due to cash flow problems you didn't even know they were having. One day you have money in the bank. You've almost saved up enough for a down payment on a home, and then disaster strikes. Someone in your family requires expensive medical care and only a fraction of it is covered by your health insurance . . . if you even *have* health insurance. One day, you have a nice home. The next day, it's wiped out by a natural disaster and you discover there was some fine-print rider on your homeowner's policy that means the damage isn't covered. Maybe the primary breadwinner is stricken with a chronic illness and can't work anymore. Maybe the interest rates on a variable mortgage become so high that you can't make your payments anymore. Maybe you were already living paycheck to paycheck and an emergency like your car breaking down makes enough of a dent in your budget that you won't be buying groceries this month. There are enough horror stories about sudden economic disasters on a personal level to fill a book, but needless to say, money problems can happen to anyone. I know this because I've been there more than once.

## My Advent into Frugality, Cheapskatery, and Thrift

My childhood was one of privilege. My mother stayed home with me, my father was a doctor, and money was never, ever a problem. When I became an adult, I never expected money to be a problem. So, you can imagine my shock when my husband lost his job when our brand-new baby girl was only one month old. We were waiting for unemployment insurance to kick in while he desperately sought a job. The area we lived in was economically depressed, however, and there was no work to be found. He picked up some work in the fields during harvest season, but aside from that, we went several months with no other income.

And it was terrifying. We spent a month eating nothing but frozen bagels that I had bought on sale, the small amount of produce we coaxed from our vegetable garden, and a monster tub of peanut butter. I washed out diapers in the tub because we didn't have a washer and dryer in our apartment, and we couldn't afford to go to the laundromat. One day, I "splurged" and picked up a book by a lady named Amy Dacyczyn for $2 at a library sale. At the time, I had no idea that that book was going to change my life. I was just hoping for a few tips to help us get by. But *The Tightwad Gazette* continues to influence me more than twenty years later.

We made it through that rough spot, but life doesn't just turn around and become perfect forevermore for most of us. During good times, we tend to relax our frugal efforts, and when a financial downturn hits, we have to get back into the mentality. I was equipped to deal with tough times until the biggie happened. When I became a single mom working a low-paying job, we got by. We ate a lot of macaroni and cheese, but we did okay. When I got laid off for a few months during a slow period at work, we lived off our pantry and handled everything with aplomb. But the year I turned forty, a series of events so awful occurred that everything in my life changed. My dad, one of the most wonderful people you could ever meet, got sick. I had a terrible feeling that this was it for him, and unfortunately, I was right. I took time off work; I spent lots of money traveling back and forth from Canada to Memphis, Tennessee, where he was hospitalized for several months, to spend every moment I could with him. When he passed away, I was devastated. Nothing in my life before or since has been so terrible.

When we returned home after the funeral, I went back to work—for a few weeks. This was during the last big economic crisis, and when my company downsized, I was one of the casualties. I no longer had the money to dump into a side business I had begun (but neglected during my father's illness).

We had been living frugally in comparison to many people, but not frugally enough to counteract that personal economic disaster. Looking back, I'm not sure if any amount of frugality could have really made a difference. (That's something else we'll talk more about—sometimes things so financially devastating occur that they can't be prevented even if you are the epitome of thrift.) We became even more thrifty of a necessity, and I deeply resented the need to do so every single time I stepped into a mall, purchased groceries, or emptied my bank account to keep the utilities on and a roof over our heads. There was nothing extra left over for fun, or even secondary needs. It was a very grim time for our family.

Within a few months, I had lost my house to foreclosure, my car to repossession, and my business due to a lack of operating capital. I didn't want to go anywhere for fear that I would run into somebody I knew, and they'd look at me with scorn, or even worse, with pity. Every material thing we had was gone except a few pieces of furniture, the laptop from my business, and my books. When the depression began to lift, I saw that getting out from under that mountain of monthly bills had actually provided me with a gift of enormous freedom. I realized that my life could take a different turn. I was no longer tied to *anything*. And that's when I began to embrace my cheap side. I loved it like a long-lost child who had come back to Mama's arms. I became what I called a Frugalite and I loved it. I realized that I no longer needed to buy into the systemic debt that had been the source of my personal economic disaster. By being as self-sufficient as possible, by cutting my spending, and by not needing "the system," I was winning. I was becoming truly free.

## Why I *Love* Words like Thrift, Frugality, and Cheapskatery

For some people, these words have negative connotations. But I think those people are wrong. Being thrifty, cheap, or frugal doesn't mean that you are miserly, non-generous, or poor. These words mean that you are thoughtful about how you spend your money. They mean that you aren't wasteful. They mean that you will creatively find a way to solve more problems with less money. They mean you are *free*. You are way freer than the folks who spend money before they make it and who are mired in debt. If you are a full-fledged Frugalite, you are free from:

- Financial fear
- Overwhelming debt

- Constant work to keep up with your expenses
- Giving half a hoot about what the "Joneses" are doing

Here's what these words do *not* mean. Thrift, in all but the direst of situations, doesn't mean that you have to live a spartan life with boring food, no Internet, and only productive hobbies while wearing mismatched second-hand clothing. You can travel, eat out at nice restaurants, play Yahtzee with the neighbors, go to the movies, and shop for nice clothing as long as you can make it fit your financial plan. You can reach crazy goals that nobody would ever imagine that somebody with your budget would be able to reach. It's your choice—cut what is unnecessary and spend where you decide. I hope that you will embrace thrift, frugality, and cheapskatery as much as I have. It will change your life in the most glorious ways.

## About This Book

This book started off as a monthly newsletter that was an homage to my beloved Amy Dacyczyn. (Yes, I adore her, No, I haven't met her, and she probably has no earthly idea who I am.) Her books, compiled together in *The Complete Tightwad Gazette*, were instrumental in helping me get my financial poop together. In fact, I recommend you hop onto wherever you order your books and get yourself a copy right now to read the moment you are finished with this. After writing the newsletter for a year, I decided that putting this stuff into a format that people could revisit annually would be a good idea.

Thus, this book was born.

I hope that this book will change the way you look at money—not having it, spending it, and saving it. Frugality can actually be fun, it can make your life fulfilling and free from stress, and best of all, it can make your dreams come true.

Let's get thrifty!

# Part One
# A Frugal State of Mind

Let's define frugal living. And not just everyday plain old thrifty. I'm talking about the ultimate level of epic cheapskatery. I'm talking about being a card-carrying member of Clan Frugalite. (It's not for sissies.) Hardcore frugality is not just making a choice to buy the generic brand of laundry soap instead of a jug of Tide with scent beads. Hardcore frugality is buying the ingredients to make five times the amount of laundry soap for half the price of that name-brand detergent, all the while *loving* the fact that the execs at Procter & Gamble are not going to their annual retreat in Santorini on your money.

You have begun to embrace your cheap side when you can cross that line between *resenting* the fact that you have to strictly budget to *welcoming* the fact that by being as frugal as possible, you have a freedom you never dreamed of before. Earning your black belt in frugality takes creativity and an optimistic outlook. It should never be some grim, sad thing that you have to do. It should be something that you choose to do. By finding joy in your non-consumerism, you will be far more successful at it. It becomes a game that you win if you can do something for free that others spend money on. When you feel like you require less, you are happy with less. This means that you have to spend less time working at things you may not truly enjoy so that you can pay for the things you never actually needed in the first place. This means that the money you do have goes a lot further.

## It's All about Your Attitude

As a parent, sometimes I've asked my kids to do things they don't want to do. (Haven't we all?) The biggest key to their success in the endeavor is their attitude.

**Scenario #1:**

**Me**: "Kiddo, it's time to swap your winter clothes for your spring clothes. Please go through your closet, sort through your winter clothes, and get rid of the stuff that's too small or that you don't want anymore."

**Kiddo**: "I don't want to! I hate this! It's not fair!"

Kiddo goes through the closet, angrily shoving things in a garbage bag without taking a good hard look at things. She sulks, pouts, and is otherwise miserable. She gets the job done but makes sure that it is unpleasant for *all* of us.

**Scenario #2:**

**Me**: "Kiddo, it's time to swap your winter clothes for your spring clothes. Please go through your closet, sort through your winter clothes and get rid of the stuff that's too small or that you don't want anymore."

**Kiddo**: "Okay—this gives me a chance to see if there's anything I can repurpose, too!"

Kiddo goes through the closet, eagerly sorting items into piles. She comes up with a good stash of "new" materials for craft projects, a bag of donations, and two shirts that were buried at the back that she forgot she had. The job is done, and the end result is its own reward.

Switching over to a more frugal lifestyle can be just like the above scenarios. You can embrace it and relish the challenge of it, or you can sulk, pout, and be absolutely miserable. At this point in my life, things are no longer as hard as they were before. But still, I *choose* to live a frugal life. I opt to live a frugal, non-consumer lifestyle because of my personal experiences. Disengaging from the uncaring financial machine has provided me with a freedom I never had when I was spending close to six figures while earning twenty times that for a corporation that cared only about the bottom line. Even if you're doing okay financially, living frugally can allow you to do outrageous things that you technically shouldn't be able to afford on your paycheck, like traveling the world, living in a paid-off home, or putting your children through college debt-free.

## 7 Steps to the Joy of Frugal Living

If you're coming over to the cheap side, you need to embrace it. You need to play it like a game you are determined to win and cheer yourself on like you're in the last quarter of a Final Four playoff. That will keep you motivated during the good times and propel you through the rough times. These 7 steps will help you keep your head right.

**1. Be grateful.** An "attitude of gratitude" is the most vital part of embracing your cheap side. If you're happy with what you've got, you will find that you "need" far less than you did before. That's because you aren't seeking some momentary hit of joyous adrenaline by purchasing something. That rush rarely lasts and you're just left with more stuff and less money.

**2. Be creative.** How can you make something, save something, or repair something in a totally original way? Embrace the challenge and tap into your creativity. You may just discover that, in your originality, you've come up with something far better than the purchased alternative. (We've found this to be especially true with fashion accessories, home décor, and birthday parties!)

**3. Give.** Frugality doesn't mean you're stingy. There are always people who are worse off than you. It's important to give a hand up to those people. If your kids were hungry or cold or without shelter, wouldn't you hope that some kind person would help them? Even at our absolute rock bottom financially, we donated one can of spaghetti sauce and a package of noodles to the food bank every week, which hopefully provided one warm, comforting meal for someone who needed it. My girls chose those sauces and noodles with the care of a Cordon Bleu chef picking ingredients. It isn't necessary to debate whether people are truly in need or just milking the system. That is a subject for them and their consciences. Just give when you can. You are responsible for your intentions, not theirs.

**4. Spend your money where it really matters.** When things were at their worst for us, we opted to move to a very small community into a drafty little cabin in the woods. We made this decision as a family in order to reduce our monthly output. By getting rid of "city rent" and all of the bills that came with it, we cut our monthly output in half. This means that I was able to start a business without having a ton of overhead to cover. When my daughter needed new glasses, it was not a problem to pay for them. It meant my older daughter could get through college without crippling student loans even while I was making less than $30,000 a year.

**5. Less need equals more time.** Not only does a thrifty lifestyle mean that I can refocus where my money goes. It means that I can refocus where my time goes. I don't have to work quite as hard on stuff outside the home and can focus on home and family. I have the time to make hats and scarves instead of purchasing them. I have time to garden and preserve the harvests. I have time to perform money-saving tasks like cooking from scratch, which goes into that big happy circle of having more money to put toward important things. This isn't to say you can only live a frugal life by crocheting mittens and growing tomatoes—we all have our own frugal path to find. Your talents and patience may lie in other directions than mine. Life changes constantly as well. During a summer with lots of travel, my canned goods might come from the farmers' market. During a phase with book deadlines, dinner might come from the grocery store with a $5 rotisserie chicken (cheaper than I can make at home) and a can of green beans.

**6. Hang out with like-minded people.** It is so much easier to embrace your cheap side if you don't have people telling you how deprived you are all the time or berating you for being too cheap to spend $27.85 on a movie ticket, popcorn, and a soda. Most of my closest friends are thrifty. We swap clothing, we borrow and lend tools, and we cheerfully hang out without spending a dime. Instead of heading to the mall, we chat on Skype. Instead of going out to sit in a coffee shop sipping a $6.00 latte with whipped cream, we sit in the garden at one of our houses sipping a coffee that one of us made, along with a homemade blueberry muffin. We enjoy the same conversation we would have had at that coffee shop, too. When your nearest and dearest are on the same page, life is a whole lot easier.

**7. Turn off the TV.** People go to school for years to study how to make people want what they don't need. That great big brainwash box sitting in the living room is a direct pipeline into your mind. From the beautiful homes on the TV programs, the fancy clothes, and the ads for food, recreation, and new cars, the whole racket is designed to make you feel that what you have now is inferior to what you *could* have. Kids are the biggest target of product placement advertising in popular shows. If you watch TV, limit it. Become aware of the scams and discuss them with your kids so that they can easily identify how marketers are attempting to manipulate them. Also, lest it sounds like we sit around by candlelight singing Kumbaya, we do stream some shows in our home. But when we do, it's a big game to identify the hidden ads. While this may sound contrary to my advice to turn the TV off, I believe that some limited viewing coupled with an awareness of marketing techniques inoculates my children against the sales pitch. Also, if you have decent Internet, streaming is a kabillion times cheaper than cable and often has no commercials.

## Living *beneath* Your Means

While many people advocate living within your means, I don't think that's necessarily enough. I'm a proponent of living *beneath* one's means. Within is great, because it signifies a lack of debt and only spending what you can afford. But beneath is even better, because it signifies that you have quite a bit left over for dealing with a rainy day.

Living beneath your means may not sound like a whole lot of fun. It sounds as though a person doing this is stuffing coffee cans full of dollar bills into spaces in the walls, darning socks until they simply can't withstand another repair, and eating cold beans in a darkened room to save on the electric bill. In reality, it isn't like that at all. Learning to live beneath your means can bring you a kind of peace that you never felt before. It can help you survive financial crunches both large and small. It can teach you to take joy in simpler things instead of always looking for the next expense that will give you a surge of endorphin-laced happiness.

If this is elementary to you, hang in there because there are graduate level frugality ideas on the way. We're starting off with the fundamentals and will move on toward high-level, PhD thrift from there. Some have gotten themselves into a pickle and want to figure out a way to get out of it. Others have already cut down to the bare bones and are still having trouble. Either way, if you want to live the cheap life, you're going to need to make some radical changes.

## The Frugalite's Quick-Start Spending Freeze

Want to know how to get started on your life of epic cheapskatery? It's easy. Stop spending money. *Duh.* No joke. But you see, most people spend money every single day. I'm not talking about your day-to-day necessities like house payments and fuel for the vehicle. I'm talking about those little impulse buys that most of us make without thinking twice about them. We spend more money than we realize on silly things. If you spend money on the following, you could go a lot longer than you think without spending.

- Drive-through coffee
- Delivery or takeout pizza
- Lunches out with friends from work
- Buying a drink while you are out
- Buying magazines
- Going for manicures/pedicures/facials
- Driving places just to have something to do

It's these little things that add up and can take an enormous chunk out of your budget. We've become a nation of consumers who think nothing of plunking down five times the value for something because we're out and it's convenient. Instead of the above, you could make some small one-time investments and . . .

- Bring your own coffee in a big thermos from home
- Make pizza from scratch
- Organize a workplace potluck
- Keep a small cooler in your vehicle with drinks from home
- Read online
- Change to a simpler beauty regimen
- Stay home

By doing this, you could save thousands of dollars per year. Let me be clear: I'm not saying we should never have a treat. When my family lived in the boondocks, we'd go out on a major supply shopping trip once a month, and we'd often grab a coffee out when we did so. That day was our big outing and picking something up then was a treat. That's because a treat is, by definition, something outside the norm. When you do something every single day, it's no longer a treat, it's a habit (and an expensive one in this case).

Consider these big questions: How deeply ingrained is your spending habit? Could you institute a personal spending freeze for an entire week? For a month? How long could you go without spending money? The act of spending itself is a habit. If you can break the habit of thoughtless spending, you'll be much further ahead. You can put that money toward large investment purchases that you never realized you could afford. If you saved $1,300 in Starbucks spending, at the end of the year you could make one large purchase that could help your family be in a better position. You could go on a vacation. You could pay off some debt. Now imagine what you could do if you corralled all of your frivolous spending. Prices are going up, incomes are staying the same, and jobs are getting lost and not replaced. I'd rather these things be my choice, not just the effect of a personal financial downturn. Here's how to start a spending freeze:

**First, give yourself an allowance.** That's right, give all of the people in your family who spend money an allowance. Make it cash, and collect the bank cards, credit cards, etc. This doesn't mean that purchases cannot be made, but it will take some effort to do so, and that effort will give you time to think it through. Do you really need that pair of shoes to match that one outfit in your closet? You know, that outfit you wear once every two years? By giving yourself a little cool-off time, you're less likely to make regrettable purchases that just don't add enough value to your life. By having your spending money in cash, you have a very tangible way to see how much you've spent, and can limit the amount of frivolous spending that any family member can do. Your goal should be to finish the week with a little money left over, instead of ending the week trying to dip into next week's money.

**Pay for the essentials.** Do you want to get started on your spending freeze?
- Make a careful list and plan your meals, three per day, for the next week.
- Fill up your car with gas and put aside cash for more gas if you use more than a tank per week.
- Pay your bills.
- Then, lock up your bank cards and credit cards and put away your cash.

Now, see how long you can go without spending anything. Nothing will make you more aware of your normal spending habits than stopping them completely. Because I work from home and have no regular place to spend money, this is a little easier for me than it is for someone who goes to work outside the home every day. But it's possible. I know, because I haven't always had this lifestyle, and as a single mom with no other financial contributions, it was a matter of survival for us. I tried to make it a game and came up with all sorts of creative ways to avoid spending money. We'd walk instead of driving, have movie night at home with stovetop popcorn when something good was on network TV, and read books from the library. Life without spending money does not have to be grim and miserable. In fact, if it's grim and miserable, you won't stick with it. Your family members will commit mutiny and you'll end up spending $99.38 at the theater for a movie and snacks.

**Turn off your "consumer" button.** It's time to stop being such a consumer. Think about that word, "consumer." It always makes me think of a horde of locusts descending on a field and picking it clean. I don't want to be one of those locusts, consuming just because something is there, until it's gone. Whatever it is you want to spend money on, you might not even need it. If you do need it, instead of buying it, try making it. Not only do you save money, but you develop skills, too. Learn to entertain yourself without spending. Teach your kids to be entertained without electronic devices. Develop hobbies that are productive instead of expensive.

**How long can you go?** If you put yourself and your family on a personal spending freeze, how long could you go? Can you go for an entire week without spending money? An entire month? This spending freeze will give you a foundation for the other changes you're about to make. It may be hard, but I know you can do it. You've got this. I have faith in you.

# Part Two

## Look at the Money, Honey

How often do you hear people talk about how they would live their dreams if they only had a bit more money? People always dream about staying home with the kids or about relocating to their favorite city or traveling to some exotic locale, but often feel that these things are financially unreachable.

Do you do this yourself? If so, then maybe it's time to take a good hard look at your finances and enact a personal austerity plan to radically cut expenses. Because for many of us, the money is there. We're just spending it somewhere else. Most people would be surprised at the changes that can be made when they rethink the definition of the word "necessities."

If you want to be somewhat immune to any future financial catastrophe or want to plan for some outrageous goal, you need to perform a financial makeover to pare down the monthly output to the bare minimum. This might sound kind of grim, but it's actually not! Decreasing your monthly output provides a different kind of safety net. You can end (or at least reduce) your servitude to the system, where the government helps itself to around 30 percent of your paycheck through payroll deductions. You can make a change that allows one parent to stay home with the kids (if that's your goal). You can "just say no" to unreasonable work demands, extra projects for your boss, and long hours spent making someone else wealthy. With your new-found freedom, you may discover that you have the money to start a business, relocate, or cut back your work hours and spend more time doing the important things in life.

If your family suffered devastating financial changes, wouldn't you prefer to make the cuts now and adjust accordingly, instead of having them forced upon you through evictions, foreclosures, repossessions, and other painful methods? Trust me—it's a whole lot better to make the decision yourself. The first step is to figure out the difference between a need and a want.

## Redefining Necessities

If your finances are out of control, the best possible reality check is taking a stark look at what necessities really are. Despite what the media (and your kids) will tell you, it is actually *not* necessary to have a cell phone for each family member, a vehicle in both stalls of your two-car garage, or for your children to all have separate bedrooms. People in Venezuela, Greece, Argentina, and parts of the world that have suffered through a financial collapse will tell you that "necessities" are those things essential to life:

- Water
- Food (and the ability to cook it)
- Medicine and medical supplies
- Basic hygiene supplies
- Shelter (including utilities like lights and heat)
- Serviceable, climate-appropriate clothing (not a giant walk-in closet full—just the basics)
- Sanitation
- Self-reliance items like seeds and simple tools

Absolutely everything above those basic necessities is a luxury. Now, stick with me here. I'm not going to suggest you take a vow of poverty and dress solely in clothing made from discarded flour sacks. But we have to get down to the nitty-gritty.

**By the definition above, what luxuries do you have?**
Some luxuries are more important than others, based on your lifestyle, and might be considered secondary necessities. You might require transportation, work clothing, a computer with Internet connection, electrical appliances, a cell phone—you are the only person who can define which of these are luxuries, and which are secondary necessities. It's essential to be truly honest with yourself and separate "wants" and "I really enjoy having this" and "the kids will complain without it" from "needs."

For example, I'm a blogger. Without an Internet connection and a laptop, I have no work. For me to make a living, therefore, my computer and monthly Internet bills are necessities. However, because I work from home, a fashionable work wardrobe is not important to me. I can wear jeans and a T-shirt to work every single day (or pajamas, if I'm being honest) and it won't affect my career at all. But if you work a job in customer service, then perhaps a computer and Internet connection would be less important than a professional wardrobe.

**Here's how it all went down for me.**
I touched on this briefly earlier in the book but let me give you the down and dirty details. When I lost my job, I began looking for ways to make money from home. I was fortunate and picked up some freelance jobs pretty quickly, but I realized that I couldn't make ends meet with what I was earning, at least not in my then-current location. I knew that the nice house in the city and the late model car were no longer maintainable. When things began going downhill for me, I had to make my austerity plan in a hurry. I didn't have the luxury of a long time to prepare. We were in dire straits already when I made the decision to radically reduce my expenses.

I began to cut expenses as quickly as possible. Some of them were forced on me—we lost our home to foreclosure and our car to repossession. I simply couldn't pay for them anymore, so I began a search for a less expensive place to live. The beauty of what I do for a living is that I can live just about anywhere—I only require a reliable connection to the Internet. Within a short period of time, we'd located a very distant, very remote little cabin in the Algonquin forest of Ontario, Canada. We sold a bunch of stuff and then packed up the rest and relocated seven hours north to the boondocks, a move that saved more than a whopping $1,100 per month when compared to city life. And, friends, I went Ninja Frugalite. Although these changes were not incredibly popular with the kiddos, I made them ruthlessly.

- ✓ Moved from a four-bedroom home in the city to a small two-bedroom in a remote area (sharing a room—oh, the humanity!)
- ✓ Cut out cable and home phone
- ✓ Provided a very limited budget to the kids for school clothes, winter coats, and holiday gifts. If something "better" was wanted, they had to earn the difference
- ✓ Made the kids do extra chores for privileges like field trips, vacations, and houseguests

✓ Began cooking entirely from scratch and limiting meals out to birthdays or long trips

✓ Began gardening, preserving bulk foods, and shopping through mail order sources

I paid $900 cash for an old truck with four-wheel drive and we left the city with a spirit of adventure. With white knuckles, I drove the U-Haul myself and towed my truck. This was the first time I ever a) drove anything as big as a U-Haul and b) towed anything. But when you're committed to radical change, you'll do all sorts of crazy things you've never done before. And the feeling of satisfaction is like no other. Only one year later, my oldest daughter headed off to college on a scholarship and Mama's dime with nary a student loan in sight.

**You can change your life, too.**

I realize that the changes I made are not changes that will work for everybody. I'm not suggesting the changes are always a whole lot of fun either. But almost everyone has some places they can make dramatic cuts—if they're willing.

Adjusting your own situation requires a brutal analysis of your expenditures. If you can't get your partner or spouse on board, it's much more difficult to do a complete overhaul. If you're in that situation, overhaul the things you can control in the hopes that your significant other will decide "Hey, that's pretty cool." Kids, however, must deal with it. Expect loud complaints but be firm. You are the parent.

I became financially independent *after* a job loss, *after* a foreclosure, and *after* a car repo. I was a formerly flat-broke single mom paying for the debt-free education of a kid in college and homeschooling another kid. If I can do this, *so can you.* At least, you can if you really, truly want it.

## First Things First: You Need an Emergency Fund

What would happen if you missed a paycheck? What would it mean to you if you had an unexpected trip to the emergency room? If your car required an expensive repair? What if your fridge that you just stocked with groceries gasped its last breath? What if your income was interrupted for a week, or two weeks, or even longer? Do you have an emergency fund built into your budget to see you through these everyday calamities? Or are you only one missed paycheck away from disaster? Because these things happen, and they happen regularly.

According to a 2020 survey released by Bankrate,[1] 59 percent of Americans do not have the emergency savings to take care of a crisis that costs $1,000 or more. How do people handle unexpected expenses? According to the survey:

- 41 percent would use savings
- 16 percent would use credit cards
- 14 percent would borrow from friends or family
- 13 percent would reduce other spending to cover the expense
- 7 percent would take out a personal loan

Many said they had no idea how they would cover an unexpected expense of this magnitude. So, what about you? Do you have an emergency fund? It needs to be part of your budget. And not something you tack on at the end. The *first* part.

## An emergency fund is vital.

When your finances are tight, sometimes your first impulse is to spend every dime. Many people focus on things like paying off debts, stocking up on food and supplies, or paying more than the minimum payments on bills. However, that may not always be your best bet.

Don't get me wrong, paying off debt is vital, but most experts recommend establishing an emergency fund as the first step back to financial security. There are several reasons why this should be a priority for you:

- What if you suddenly lost your job and it was six to eight weeks before unemployment payments began to trickle in?
- What if your child suffered a medical emergency and you needed to purchase an expensive medication or pay for treatment?
- What if your refrigerator began making a death rattle and you needed to buy a new one immediately to save your expensive frozen food stockpile?
- What if your car, that you need to get back-and-forth to work, required a costly repair?

---

1   Amanda Dixon, "Survey: Nearly 4 in 10 Americans Would Borrow Money to Cover a $1K Emergency," Bankrate, Jan. 22, 2020, https://www.bankrate.com /banking/savings/financial-security-january-2020/

The reasons you might need to tap into an emergency fund are as varied as the news headlines—there are many different personal disasters that can arise, and nearly every single one of them will require that you have some additional funds available. You simply cannot call yourself "financially prepared" if you don't have currency on hand to see you through the rough spots. Saving it isn't that much fun, but having it when you need it is the best feeling ever.

A word of warning here: don't let your short-term emergency become a long-term problem. It's important *not* to rely on credit cards, overdraft, and lines of credit for these unexpected events—those methods will cost you far more in interest in the long run. Credit cards are *not* an emergency fund. An emergency fund is *currency that you have on hand that will not cost you interest*. Don't make your personal disaster worse than it already is by paying compounded interest on it for the next two years.

**How much should be in your emergency fund?**
This is one of those numbers that will vary with different families. Most experts recommend a starting point of one to three months of expenses. And by expenses, I mean everything from house payments to car payments to projected utilities to food costs. Don't underestimate how much it takes to run your household every month. Be sure to account for all of the regular expenses you might need to cover during an emergency situation.

In addition to an emergency fund in cash, necessary items that you keep on hand can help see you through a rough spot. A stockpile of general supplies and a pantry full of bargain-priced food means you have to spend less money on day-to-day items when times are tough. Check out my book *Prepper's Pantry* for more ideas on this. (Trust me, you'll love it even if you aren't getting ready for the zombie apocalypse.)

**How to bankroll your emergency fund when times are tight.**
If you don't have some rainy-day money set aside, it is of the utmost importance that you fund this right away. It's time to change your financial lifestyle. Hardcore frugality is the answer. If you don't have enough money set aside to weather a crisis, then you need to cut your spending to the bone until you do.

- **Most of us have some places that we can cut the budget**.
  To put it into perspective, a fancy frozen coffee-like concoction from

Starbucks is about $6. A workweek without Starbucks = $30 in the bank. A month = $120. More on budget-cutting coming up.

- **Sell something.** Do you have a basement full of unused relics? Exercise equipment, old furniture, unused appliances—all these things taking up valuable storage real estate can help you to establish your emergency fund.

- **Get a second job.** You don't have to plan to work two jobs indefinitely but spending one day a week babysitting or taking on a part-time job can help you get your savings into the comfort zone.

- **Make only your minimum payments.** I realize this is not the standard financial recommendation, but until you have a one-month rainy day fund set aside, you should forgo making the extra payments even on interest-bearing accounts.

- **Eat cheap for a few months.** If you can manage one cheapo meal a day, this can result in massive savings. Consider different meals that are less than a dollar per serving—generally these will be vegetarian offerings like beans and rice, a bowl of cereal, or eggs and toast. Soup is also a great budget-stretcher. And for the love of puppies, don't eat out—the cost per serving is five to ten times the cost of making the same dish at home.

- **Get rid of some fixed expenses.** If you can get rid of some of your monthly fixed expenses, you can build your emergency fund very quickly. Cancel gym memberships, extracurricular activities, phones, satellite, cable, and Internet. Funnel all of that money toward your emergency fund.

Once the fund is built, you may discover you didn't really need those services or things as much as you thought you did.

**What constitutes an "emergency" worthy of dipping into the fund?**
Once you have your emergency fund established, you might wonder "What can I spend this on?" Ideally, nothing. The goal is to *never* spend this money. This little safe full of money squirreled away is there for situations that cannot be addressed with your regular income.

Here are some things that are ***not emergencies***:

- Trips to the mall
- Concert tickets

- Vacations
- Your 346th pair of shoes
- A celebratory dinner at a nice restaurant
- Cell phone bill (unless it's your family's only phone in which case it might be worthy of the fund)

Ask yourself a few questions to determine if the emergency is worthy of dipping into your carefully accumulated fund.

- Will it cost me more money if I do this later rather than sooner?
- Is the expenditure related to a safety issue?
- Is the expenditure related to a health issue?
- When will I have the money to pay for this out of my regular income?

Here are some examples of emergency spending that may not be able to wait.

- Refrigerator
- Car repair
- Medication/medical bill
- Washing machine (not in all situations, but if you have a baby in cloth diapers it's pretty vital!)
- Utility bills that will result in reinstatement charges

Only you can judge whether or not an event constitutes an emergency. If you must use money from your emergency fund, make it a priority to replace that withdrawal as quickly as possible.

It may seem counterintuitive to start an emergency fund when you're swimming in debt, but this is the very first step toward greater financial security. Go ahead—squirrel away $25 to $50 for a rainy day from each paycheck. Consider having it withdrawn from your pay automatically and you may not even miss it.

**Now, it's time for a cold, hard dose of personal economic reality.** Are you ready? Are you motivated? Do you want to stop living paycheck to paycheck? Let's rock and roll.

## Where Are Your Finances at Right Now?

You can't get to where you're going if you don't know where you are. And, if you don't know where you are right now, it's time to find out. Warning: it may not be at all pleasant. But like digging out a deeply lodged splinter, it's necessary to feel some pain to improve the situation. Just take a deep breath and get 'er done.

How do you do most of your spending? If it's with your debit card, it will be pretty easy to get started immediately. Simply print out your records for the last two months, and then move on to the next step. (If you spend a mixture of money from your bank account and cash that you have on hand, you may have to get a notebook and start tracking your spending, then move on to the next step in a couple of weeks.) It's vital to note every single dime that you spend. Like a leaky faucet in a bathroom few people use, it's those tiny but consistent drips that add up to an astonishing number of gallons of waste.

**Now, organize your spending into categories.**

I use categories, then subcategories:

**1. Fixed Expenses:** These are expenses that don't change from month to month, like: mortgage, rent, property taxes, cable bill, car payment, insurance. You can then break these down into two subcategories:
- Necessities
- Optional expenses

**2. Variable Expenses:** These expenses can be adapted to fit your financial situation, and sometimes even eliminated if necessary: food, utilities, clothing, gasoline, entertainment. (Obviously the need for things like food can't be eliminated, but you can spend more or less money when adjustments are needed.) Again, we can break these into subcategories based on how vital they are:
- Necessities
- Optional expenses

All of your spending will fall into these categories and subcategories.

*Now please don't misunderstand. There's absolutely nothing wrong with a little bit of luxury spending that you've budgeted for, as long as it doesn't put you behind on necessary spending. My family and I get new clothes, take vacations, and go out to dinner from time to time—we just make sure the spending works within the confines of our budget.*

Here's a mistake to avoid. Don't say to yourself "Well, I usually don't spend $400 on clothing so that isn't realistic." If you spent it, then it's realistic. You are averaging together two months, which should account for those less common expenses. Brutal honesty isn't fun, but it's vital for this exercise.

On another piece of paper, write down your income from all sources:

- Jobs
- Rental properties you may own
- Child support
- Alimony
- Settlements or debt repayment
- Any other money you have coming in on a reliable basis

Only write down regular sources of income for this exercise. Things like tax returns or one-time sales don't count toward this exercise.

Balance your total spending with your monthly income.

**How does your output compare to your income?**
You'll find yourself in one of a few different situations:

- If you aren't good at tracking your expenditures, you may have income that is unaccounted for. For example, maybe you have no actual money left over, but there is $300 that you can't account for. Put this in your miscellaneous category, since you obviously spent it.
- You are breaking even and maybe even putting some money in savings.
- You are breaking even with nothing left over.
- You are spending more than you are bringing in, and you're using credit to support a lifestyle you can't afford.

- You can't pay all of your bills, your credit is either maxed out or nonexistent, and you can barely keep the lights on and a roof over your head.

So, where do you stand in all of this? Are you in better shape or worse shape than you thought? Many of us are shocked every time we do this exercise—and I say every time because it's something you should do more than once. Little things sneak in when times are good. You need to perform regular audits of your spending, even once you've gone over to the cheap side.

Hang on to this piece of paper, because we'll use this to create a shiny new budget.

**Next, establish your minimum for living expenses.**
For this calculation, first add up your fixed necessities. This is the amount you need to keep a roof over your head, your car in the driveway, and any other regular payments that you make to keep those two things going.

Then, add up your variable necessities. There's some wiggle room here, because we can always dial back our groceries, the amount that we drive our vehicles, etc., but we have to add some of this in to our calculations.

Add these two amounts together. In a financial worst-case scenario, this is the minimum amount of money that you need to maintain some semblance of your current lifestyle. This amount needs to be set aside each month before another penny is spent. Everything you have on top of this is gravy.

**Now, it's time to make a *real* budget.**
Budget is a b-word, but it isn't a dirty one. It's actually okay even though people shudder and think of deprivation. Think of it as a diet for your finances. Just like a diet for your health, it can be a bit difficult, but the end results are worth it. Now that you have the whole picture in your sweaty little hand, it's time to go in like Jack the Ripper on a foggy night and do some slashing.

When you look at your piece of paper with your average monthly expenditures for the past two months, some things will leap out at you. Are there any surprises? Did you actually realize how much you had been spending? Are there any expenditures that are shockingly high for something that is unimportant? Your first step is to see where you can cut things out right now from the above expenditures.

We're going to look at three different categories of expenditures:

- **Fixed expenses:** These are the regular expenditures that come out of your account every single month: mortgage, car payment, taxes, insurance, cable, phone bill—you get the idea.
- **Variable expenses:** These are (usually) small, incidental expenses that you don't even think about because "it's only a few bucks." They can really add up over the course of the year and can make huge changes to your budget.
- **Debt:** Debt can be secured or revolving. For the purposes of this book, we're mostly focusing on revolving debt. Not many families are able to go out and plunk down $20,000 for a reliable car or $200,000 for a home.

Now, let's see where we can cut some money, shall we?

## Variable Expenses

The place many people can slash money ruthlessly is in their variable expenses. These can be big or small. They are often little random expenditures that siphon away money subtly. The $5 here and $10 there. Depending on how you spend, that $5 could be $150—this is all relative to how you spend money. These are expenses that can change from month to month, unlike things like rent or car payment. It's a great place to do two things:

1. Make lots of easy adjustments
2. Get yourself into a thrifty state of mind

When you really calculate how much these small expenditures can add up, you may be stunned at the waste. Before you say "Oh, that's only $2, it doesn't matter" think about this:

*Two dollars, saved on a daily basis over the course of a year, is $730.
If you save $2 on four different things, that total is $2,920.*

Sure, if you're a multimillionaire homeowner with a paid-off house, yacht, and car, those numbers are small potatoes. But for most of us, a savings of $2,920 makes an awfully big difference. A hefty chunk of emergency fund or paid-off debt. A wonderful purchase you never dreamed you'd be able to make.

So, stop thinking small. Think *big*. Think about what you'll save over the course of an entire year. Let's start out by talking about the small changes that can add up to huge savings for your household.

## It's the Little Things That Add Up

Let's start off with the easy stuff and look for those little random expenditures that siphon away money subtly. The $5 here and $10 there. You may have just discovered that you spend $300 to $400 each month for a daily lunch out that didn't seem like much in individual increments, but when you add the daily $5 drive-through coffees and an afternoon bottle of water, ends up exceeding $500 a month.

Half a thousand.

Lotsa money.

Maybe you smoke or drink alcohol outside the home on a regular basis. Do what you're going to do—I'm not here to tell you to stop smoking or drinking—but take a look at how much you're spending to do it. Maybe you buy a giant soda pop at the gas station every day for a couple of dollars. That adds up, too. Nearly everyone discovers that they have at least one bad spending habit in this part. Don't beat yourself up. Just fix it. Imagine what your life would be like with the money you blow on cigarettes, drive-through coffee, ~~hookers and cocaine just kidding I know you aren't like that,~~ giant fountain sodas, and happy hour tucked away waiting to help you through an emergency.

You may not want to make changes. You may not want to sacrifice your little luxuries. You may feel like you "deserve" them or that you have "earned" them. You may be digging in your heels right this very moment and saying "What does it matter if I spend a piddly $5 a day on something that gives me pleasure?" It matters. It matters a lot, especially when you add it up over the course of the year. Especially if you're living paycheck to stressful paycheck. Unless you make some changes, you won't be able to make some changes. Capisce?

Getting rid of the bad habits is probably one of the easiest ways to cut spending. Find a substitute that costs less. This can be a process. Not everything has to be cut out cold turkey, especially if you aren't in a bind. If times are tight, though, you may want to be more relentless and immediate in your cost-cutting. You may have already cut some of the following common variable expenses, but let's revisit them anyway for the newbies:

*Take-out coffee*

One report[2] said that the average American spends a whopping $1,100 a year on coffee. Honestly, I know lots of people who spend even more. Here are a few ways to conquer the coffee monster:

- Get a thermos and doctor up your coffee at home, just how you like it, with the perfect amount of cream and sugar. (A good thermos can be purchased for about the cost of a week of drive-through coffees.)
- Like flavored coffees? Learn to make your own for a fraction of the cost. (See some creamer recipes on page 125.)
- If you are too lazy to set up a pot of coffee the night before and put it on a timer, even one of those machines with the little pod things is cheaper than going to Starbucks for every single sip. (But this is *definitely* not the most frugal way to brew your coffee at home.)

You don't have to give up your coffee—just the drive-through part.

*Eating lunch out*

Bring your dang lunch to work. Brown bag it. Get one of those nifty little Bento boxes for lunch. When I worked outside the home, I packaged up leftovers every night into a container I could take to work the following day. Then, all I had to do was grab it and go in the morning. Bonus: what you bring from home is probably going to be far healthier than what you'd get at a restaurant. If you like to read, bring a book and use your lunch break as some much-needed quiet time.

However, if lunch out with your officemates is something you do every day and you're completely unwilling to give it up, you can, at the least, work on cutting the costs.

- Take a morning and afternoon snack to the office and then get something like a cup of soup at lunch, instead of a full meal.
- Drink water instead of buying a soda pop or a tea.
- Split a meal with a likeminded colleague.
- Sometimes it causes fewer questions to just say you're cutting back (you know you mean money, but they'll think you mean calories).

---

2 Acorns "Money Matters Report," p. 11, https://app.box.com/s/sikpbs94y84tdug qy3rvqu0s1mv74sr8

- See if anyone at work is interested in doing a weekly potluck with you.
- Often, the portions at restaurants are a bit more than we need anyway, so try just going with a side salad or an appetizer.

I know. Food is social and it has been since the beginning of time. But it doesn't have to kill your budget.

*Smoking*

If you're a smoker, you already know it's a terrible habit. I'm not here to tell you that you must stop immediately. That's your business. But . . . *gulp* . . . look at *how much money* you're spending! At the very least, consider cutting back. If you are a pack-a-day smoker, cut down first to six packs per week. Put the money for that extra pack into a jar because the visual can be very inspiring. The more you reduce the amount you smoke, the more money you'll save. And maybe, one of these days, it will be enough to inspire you to quit altogether.

*Drinking alcohol*

If you drink alcohol, you probably know that going out and indulging at a bar is about a million times more expensive than doing so at home. I have long since relegated alcohol consumption to special occasions only.

- If you really don't feel your day is complete without a cocktail or a glass of wine, have it at home.
- Consider limiting this to special occasions or once a week, if you go out often.
- Try making your own homebrewed wine or beer. But beware of those fancy kits—you could end up spending more than a trip to the liquor store would have been.
- You can drink but be aware of how much money you're guzzling away.

*Water*

No, I'm not suggesting that you stop hydrating, but you may be spending far more than you should to do so. Do you buy a bottle of water every time you walk into the gas station or into a store? Do you hit the vending machine at work to buy one? If so, you know that you could buy an entire case of bottled water for the cost of two to three individual ones.

- **BYOB:** I never leave home without a water bottle in my hand.
- **Filter your tap water:** If you're like me, you aren't a fan of the chemicals in city water. If you get a good quality water filter rated to remove chemicals like chlorine and fluoride, fresh water can be yours for only the cost of filter changes.
- **Refill 5-gallon jugs with purified water:** This is a cost-effective way to purchase water.
- **Stash cases of water:** Keep them in your car and in your office to quench your thirst.
- **Pick up a small water cooler for your office:** After the initial investment, it will cost you pennies compared to what you spent before.

And speaking of water . . .

## Drink water.

It's entirely possible that you are blowing a ton of money drinking other beverages when you could simply drink water. Even if you purchase it in 5-gallon jugs with the hot/cold dispenser, it's still the best deal around, with the added bonus of being good for your health. Coffee, lemonade, and tea that you make at home are also very inexpensive. Skip the soda pop, juices, milk, and sports drinks. Also, skip the individual bottles of water because those can be almost as pricey as buying a soda.

If you have children, you are not doing them a disservice by giving them water to drink. In fact, you are teaching them one of the healthiest habits around by encouraging them to enjoy pure, fresh water when they're thirsty. Obviously, if you have toddlers you should follow the advice of your pediatrician as far as their beverages are concerned. However, helping your child develop a taste for plain water can start early if it doesn't take the place of necessary nutrients.

You don't like water? My first thought was to say "you'll adjust" but my editor tells me that isn't nice. So, here's the nurturing answer: put some slices of fruit in it for a light flavor. Begin to dial back the fruit until you are just drinking water. You'll adjust *slowly*.

These are just a few ideas. There are many ways to save money on groceries, utilities, child-rearing, and homekeeping and we'll get into those later. The little things that you overspend on could be totally different than the ones listed above, but you can use these as inspiration for cutting your own bad-habit spending.

## Fixed Expenses

Lots of financial experts give tips about reducing your discretionary spending, but what about those fixed expenses? Some of these, you can't do anything about. However, some of these payments can be reduced or gotten rid of altogether.

Most of us have a set of fixed expenses. Some of these are vital, some are not, and what is vital for me might not be important for you. What fixed payments come out of your bank account every month?

- Mortgage/rent
- Home/car insurance
- Car payment
- Cable/satellite/Internet
- Gym membership/exercise classes
- Loan payments
- Phone bills
- Child support/alimony payments
- Tuition
- Extracurricular activities for the kids

The real question is, if your financial circumstances changed dramatically, could you afford your current lifestyle? If the answer to that question is "No" then you need to figure out how to reduce your regular monthly output. Keep in mind that what works for my family may not work for your family. It will depend on whether your spouse is on board, how dire your situation is, and with how much importance you weigh your frugality makeover. Some of these measures would be drastic, and others would only cause a minor change in your lifestyle. Let's take a look at each of these expenses individually and ask ourselves some important questions.

**1. Mortgage/rent:** This is often the biggest expenditure that many families make each month. When you buy a house, realtors will nearly always show you homes at the top of your price range. When you are looking for rentals, most people search at the high end of their budgets. That's fine in good times, but if things go awry, you're stuck at that same level because banks and landlords don't care that you lost your job or took a financial hit.

Sometimes moving to a less expensive place is your only option if you wish to make big financial changes. This can free up as much as a thousand dollars a month for some families. Moving is expensive, though, and you must figure that into the potential savings. If you are only going to save, let's say, $50 a month by moving, it will be more than a year before you recoup your expenses, and that is going to do little to change your overall outlook. If you are moving to drop your expenses, it needs to be a substantial monthly savings to make it worthwhile. If you own your home, consider refinancing at a better interest rate.

**2. Home/car insurance:** You have to have insurance, so this is not an expense that you can cut out of your budget altogether. However, you can shop around for better prices. You can look into changing your coverage. Do you have duplications in coverage? For example, my insurance company offers roadside assistance for about $40 per year, but my vehicle came with three years of free roadside assistance. You can drop your rate further by increasing your deductible, but if you do that, be sure you have access to the deductible amount in your emergency fund should an accident occur. If you have several cars in your family, you might not need to have rental car coverage on your policy.

**3. Car payment:** As with a home payment, most people push the envelope and get the nicest vehicle that they can afford. What you drive is a status symbol in North America, and practicality doesn't always come into the decisions. The best option is to get something that you can afford to pay for in full so that you don't have a payment. Consider trading in the vehicle you are making payments on for one that you can pay for outright or make payments on for a short period of time. But if you made the purchase decision in less frugal days, you might be what car dealers call "upside down" in your financing. That means you owe more on your vehicle than it is worth. If that is the case, then you will basically have to pay someone to take it off your hands, and that is not always worth your while. If you find yourself in that situation, the best thing you can do is use some of your freed-up money to pay off your loan as quickly as possible. At least then, the bank gets less interest from you.

If you have more than one vehicle, is it possible to become a one-car family? This will drop your automotive maintenance costs, get rid of an insurance payment, and take away a monthly payment if both vehicles are being financed. If one of your vehicles is paid for, consider getting rid of the one that is being financed.

**4. Cable/satellite/Internet:** This is an area in which cuts can almost always be made. We don't have cable or satellite, but we do have the best Internet available. In my home, Internet is vital for my job and was vital when I was homeschooling my daughter. Since we have Internet, if we have the urge to watch something, we can stream it online. For your entertainment needs, consider something like Netflix, Hulu, or Amazon Prime. It's a fraction of the price of a monthly cable or satellite bill and you can choose what you want to watch at any point in time, not just when it's on network television. Expect an outcry if you get rid of these services, but also know that your family will get used to it quickly. Trust me, they'll live.

**5. Gym membership/exercise classes:** Being healthy is a top priority if you want to live a frugal lifestyle, but that doesn't mean you have to accrue high monthly fees to do so. You can kill two birds with one stone by coming up with some productive active things to do: chop wood, build, garden, or farm. If you live in a place where it's reasonable to do so, walk instead of driving—you'll get some exercise while saving gas money and wear and tear on your vehicle. Go for active entertainment, too, like hiking trips or camping. The more you move your body, the better off you'll be.

**6. Loan payments:** Look at paying off your debts as quickly as possible using the snowball method. (More about that coming up.) Then, once you have no debt, commit yourself to staying that way.

**7. Phone bills:** Most people do not need both a home phone and a cell phone. One or the other will nearly always suffice. I actually went years without either one. I used Internet phone service, which cost $2.99 per month for the odd telephone call I had to make, and email for everything else. It takes some getting used to, but you might find that you welcome the peace of people being unable to interrupt you just as you sit down to dinner. Because I'm an uber-introvert, I loved it. You can free up a lot of money each month by getting rid of the phone, but expect people to look at you strangely when they ask for your number and you say "I don't have one."

**8. Child support/alimony payments:** There really isn't a lot you can do about this kind of monthly expense, nor should you in most cases. These numbers are set by the courts and you will go to jail or have assets seized if you don't make the payments. As a single mom, I can tell you that there were times when we depended on child support payments to buy our groceries, so the argument can be made that if you have children, it's your responsibility to make these payments.

**9. Tuition:** If your child is in college or a private school, tuition payments are a fixed expense that you can't really do much to reduce. You can apply for scholarships, but aside from this, the price is the price. You don't want your child to start off adult life in debt if you can help it, so if you can find a way to make these payments instead of using student loans, you are giving your son or daughter the biggest possible gift: financial freedom.

**10. Extracurricular activities for the kids:** This one really depends on your family. If your child is just killing time, then the extracurriculars may not be of high importance. On the other hand, if they are a talented athlete or budding musician, you may find this is a very worthwhile expenditure. Some families who homeschool look to extracurricular activities as a way for their kids to socialize with peers, and that is also very important. If the activity is not a serious pursuit, sometimes it can be replaced with lower-cost activities through the local community center or YMCA. Some children are really overprogrammed with an evening activity every day of the week and two on weekends. Kids need downtime and the freedom to just go outside, climb a tree, and look at the clouds floating by.

It's far better to make these changes voluntarily before you're forced to do so by circumstances. If you can reduce your fixed monthly expenditures, you're less likely to default on things that are true necessities, like keeping a roof over your head and food in the cupboards. I would prefer to control the cuts myself rather than have the decisions made for me by financial problems down the road.

## Getting Out of Debt (Maybe)

Many Americans owe so much money that they have no idea how they'll ever manage to pay it off, and Christmas just makes it worse. Even before the bills came rolling in, a survey from AJC[3] speculated that average spending in

---

3    Fiza Pirani, "Report: Americans Plan to Spend $720 Billion This Holiday Season." The Atlanta Journal-Constitution, Dec. 10, 2018, https://www.ajc.com/news /national/report-americans-plan-spend-nearly-720-billion-this-holiday-season /fi76G7ezgnYE7jUOnfwoAL/

2018 would be $1,007.24 *per person*. Because many Americans have little cash to spare, it's a safe bet that these Christmas gifts were directly added to credit card debt. Debt that is already astronomical, by the way. Household debt is over $12 trillion and climbing. Michael Snyder[4] broke it down into numbers that are easier to grasp:

> It breaks down to about $38,557 for every man, woman, and child in the entire country. So, if you have a family of four, your share comes to a grand total of $154,231, and that doesn't even include corporate debt, local government debt, state government debt, or the gigantic debt of the federal government. That number is only for household debt, and there aren't too many Americans that could cough up their share right at this moment.

And to make matters even worse, 35 percent of these indebted Americans owe money that is past due by 180 days or more. One of the best ways to lower your monthly expenses is to get yourself out of debt.

### Is paying off debt the best option?

I'm going to give some unpopular advice here. Paying off debt is *not* always the best option. It differs from case to case. Let me preface this by saying that I believe if you promise to pay a debt, paying it should absolutely be a priority. I'm not recommending that people go out and spend frivolously with no intention of paying it back. That's stealing and a horrible thing to do.

But I recognize that situations can change, and they can do so very suddenly. And if that is your situation, paying off your credit card bill may not be the best thing to do with your money. If you only owe a couple thousand dollars, by all means, getting rid of that debt is very important *if* you can still afford the essentials of life. But if you can't afford food for your family or rent for your apartment, those credit card companies are going to have to wait.

Again, *I recommend you be responsible for debts you owe*, but you may have to put off paying them back until your situation is better. If you do that, your credit will be ruined, but your life is not over when your credit is ruined. Sure,

---

4    Michael Snyder, "America the Debt Pig: We Are a "Buy Now, Pay Later" Society - And 'Pay Later' Is Rapidly Approaching," The Economic Collapse Blog, Aug. 28, 2016, http://theeconomiccollapseblog.com/archives/america-the-debt -pig-we-are-a-buy-now-pay-later-society-and-pay-later-is-rapidly-approaching

some things will be harder, but you'll still be able to survive with a low credit rating. Good credit is not like food or air or water. It isn't essential to life, and without good credit, you will develop some awesome habits like paying cash for stuff.

The rest of this chapter assumes that paying off debt *is* the best decision for your situation.

### Here's how to pay off debt quickly.
The snowball method is a snazzy little trick that can help you pay off debt as quickly and efficiently as possible. As much as I wish I could take the credit, I did not invent this. The best book I ever read about paying off debt is *The Total Money Makeover* by Dave Ramsey. You may be able to find it at your local library, but if you can't, I suggest you buy it. Even if you are struggling financially, I recommend scrimping someplace so you can purchase this book if you are trying to pay off debt and get back on your feet.

Dave recommends something called "the snowball method" for repaying debt quickly. Imagine a snowball at the top of a hill. As you roll the snowball, you pick up more snow, and the snowball gets bigger. By the time it's at the bottom of the hill, it's huge. You can do the same thing with debt by paying off the smallest bill first, then applying what you'd normally pay on that lowest bill to the next bill. Continue adding the minimum payment for each paid-off bill to the next largest one until all your debt is repaid. (This method assumes you have enough money coming in to make your basic payments, plus a little bit extra. If you're in a situation in which you truly do not have enough money to pay your bills, we will address this in the crisis mode part of the book on page 41.) I have personally used this technique to attack debt, with a few tweaks of my own.

### Here's a more detailed explanation of the snowball method.
**1. Write down every penny you owe.** It's painful but go through all your bills and write down your totals. Most people find that the total is higher than they expected. An easy way to find out exactly how much you owe, and to whom, is with a credit report. It will give you your grand totals on things like credit cards, mortgages, auto loans, etc.

**2. Organize the bills from smallest to largest amounts.** This may not seem like it makes much sense but, trust me, there's a method to the madness here.

**3. Write another list of the minimum payments for each bill.** This is your baseline of payments each month. For the sake of ease, let's say there are ten bills with a total of $750 in monthly minimum payments.

**4. Now, figure out the rest of your budget.** Once you pay your rent/mortgage, buy groceries, and pay the utility bills, how much money do you have on top of your $750 a month? For this exercise, we'll say you have an extra $100.

**5. Now, you're going to start putting all your extra money on the lowest bill each month.** So, the first month, you make all of your minimum payments, and let's say $80 extra on the smallest debt will pay it off. Then apply your leftover $20 to the next smallest bill.

**6. The following month(s), take the minimum payment from the bill you paid off, the minimum from the next smallest bill, and your extra $100 to work toward paying off the second smallest debt entirely.** Keep in mind that due to interest, your other debts will not change much at all if you are only making the minimum payment.

**7. After that, combine all of your previous minimum payments with your extra hundred dollars, plus the minimum for your now-smallest bill.** It should take you two months of snowballing to pay this off.

**And that's how you pay off consumer debt quickly.**
Do you get the idea? Instead of flailing away with minimum payments and a little extra when you can, make a concrete plan to take down debt as fast as possible. It can feel strange to only make minimum payments on the larger debts, but trust me, this is much more efficient than just paying a little extra here and there. If you get new windfalls while you're paying off debt, like tax returns or bonuses, apply them to your smallest bills.

Sometimes we get into debt due to bad decisions and sometimes it's out of desperation. If you have ever been without money for groceries or utilities, you may have used a credit card even though you knew it wasn't a good idea. Maybe you had a great income when you incurred the debt but then lost your job. There are many reasons you could find yourself way over your head. That's all in the past. Don't beat yourself up, because that's ultimately counterproductive. Just commit to getting out of debt as quickly as you can and do your best to avoid the same pitfall in the future.

## How to Adjust Your Budget When Things Change

Sudden changes in your personal finances can be cause for celebration or cause for stress. Regardless of whether the news is good or bad, these changes can have an effect on your budget. If the change is more than a one-time windfall (more on windfalls in the next section) you are going to have to make some adjustments.

### What if the change is for the worse?

Let's start off with the bad news and then move on to the good news. What should you do if your finances have suddenly changed for the worse? Maybe one of the breadwinners has become unemployed. Perhaps you have suddenly been forced to take on a large debt that is going to eat a chunk out of your monthly budget. How do you survive that when you're already living paycheck to paycheck?

This is one of the most difficult things that can happen to us. We've been moving along, sticking to our budget, and putting back a few bucks here and there for an emergency fund. Then, *boom*. In one fell swoop, we're suddenly trying to figure out what to do with a major deficit. The good news is, you *will* get through this. You've handled everything with determination thus far and you will handle this too. The bad news is, something has to change ASAP.

This is usually a painful cut. Here are a few ideas that come to mind:

- Moving someplace cheaper (not possible for everyone if you're stuck in a lease or upside down in your mortgage).
- Cutting something "fun" like activities for the kids, gym memberships, a weekly outing for dinner and a movie, or a vacation you've had planned.
- Cutting something you felt was essential like a second vehicle, private school tuition, or a phone for every family member.
- Letting something go unpaid. This is the worst feeling and the last solution but sometimes it's necessary. Sometimes, to keep a roof over your heads and food in your bellies you have to sacrifice your credit and just stop paying for something. Again, this is a last resort and you should do everything possible to prevent this from happening.

I told you—none of these are fun. But when you're faced with certain ruin, you have to grit your teeth and make difficult decisions.

### What if the change is for the better?

On a more optimistic note, what if you suddenly got a huge raise? Now you can afford horseback riding lessons for the kids, a bigger house, a new car, a tropical resort vacation . . . *wait*. This is where people usually make a fatal error in their budgets. It will feel great right now to splurge, but if some time down the road you end up facing the choices in scenario number one, there's a whole lot further to fall.

If you suddenly get this wonderful regular addition to your income, your absolute best course of action is to *not* change your lifestyle dramatically. I know. I am not the bearer of good news. It's pretty sad when you suddenly have all this money and I'm telling you to stay in your reasonably priced house with your reasonably priced car and *not* go to Tahiti next month.

But what you should really do is to take these steps:

- Pay off any debt at an accelerated rate
- Build up your emergency fund
- Pay for improvements on your current home that will save you money in the long run (like new windows, a more efficient furnace, etc.)

Wow. What a letdown. Put this in the category of "Daisy-is-no-fun-at-all." Remember though—when you started on this road to Frugalite nirvana, you did it so you could have peace of mind and stop struggling. Don't make the same mistakes that caused you to struggle in the first place when you are given an opportunity to do better.

When your budget changes, you don't have to throw all your good financial habits out the window and become a big spender. We may have made that mistake in the past, but now we know better.

### Well, gee. That's a bummer.

I know this may not have been the most inspiring thing to hear, but trust me when I tell you, this is the voice of experience speaking. I'm telling you this stuff because I have made these mistakes. I have gone out and bought a vehicle I couldn't really afford in celebration of a financial uptick. I did that instead of paying off my debt. Then, I had that debt for years *and* a vehicle with outrageous payments that I had to eventually sell at a loss.

I'm not the only person who's made mistakes like that. It's human nature. What I learned from this—and what I hope to share with you—is that we *can* do better. It's just hard when you have this wonderful new income that means you could potentially afford a Mercedes instead of a Ford. That money can change your life for the better, but not if you don't use it wisely. Be smarter than younger Daisy.

**When your finances change, here's what you need to do.**
The first thing to do when your finances change, regardless of whether it's for better or worse, is to sit down with a notebook and perform a clearheaded assessment of your exact situation. Don't splurge, don't file for bankruptcy, don't do anything until you have a clear picture. Then, formulate your plan out of knowledge, patience, and common sense, not out of panic or a celebratory high.

You've got this.

## What to Do with a Financial Windfall

Don't you love it when money "falls from the sky"? That's what I always call it when I receive a financial windfall. Money falling from the sky. It could be a really hefty tax return, a gift, or the sale of some pricey item that has been just sitting around collecting dust. But wherever it comes from, the question is still the same: What should I do with all this money?

Now, it's human nature to splurge and buy all those things you've been denying yourself in your quest to be the frugalest Frugalite in all the Galaxy. New clothes, beautiful furniture, a piece of jewelry—after all, you deserve a treat! But not so fast. You've also been working at paying off debt, building an emergency fund, etc. etc. et cetera.

That little dose of reality was kind of a bummer, huh? Trust me when I tell you that many windfalls have slipped through my fingers in the past and I have sincerely regretted it. I don't want you to regret it, so learn from my mistakes back in my spendy days!

**Here's the plan.**
First, don't do *anything* immediately. You are going to feel so bad if you go and blow it all on a new living room set and then the bills come in and you wish you had paid off your credit card instead.

Then, break it up by percentages. My usual split is 10/50/40.

**10%:** Put aside a percentage of the windfall for fun stuff. For me, it's usually 10 percent and with that money I can buy anything I want, no matter how frivolous. One of my favorite ways to spend "free" money is on an adventure. I'm more into experiences than "stuff" these days. The kids will remember that time you went to the amusement park a lot more fondly than that time you bought them yet another video game.

**50%:** Add some to your emergency fund. I usually add 50 percent straight into the fund.

**40%:** There are a couple of options for the remaining 40 percent:

- **Check your snowball list.** (You know, the one where you're paying off all your debt.) Are there some small debts you can get rid of completely?
- **Is there a bulk purchase you've been wanting to make?** One that would save you a fair bit of money if you could pay for it all up front? A side of beef or your car insurance for the next six months?
- **Is there a repair you've been putting off?** Most repairs, whether they are to cars or homes, save you more money in the long run. If you wait, you risk other systems being affected by the broken item. Then, when it completely fails and you have no choice but to repair it, your bill is far higher.

Those are just my examples. You're free, of course, to split this up however you want. But—and this may be surprising—I strongly urge you to put aside a little bit of money for fun. You work hard and you deserve a treat now and then. Having a little bit extra to enjoy from time to time will help you to stay motivated. You aren't a Spartan and life is about living. Just don't go overboard and blow the whole chunk of money!

## Setting Financial Goals and Mapping Your Plan

For me, setting a goal is the best way to keep myself on track about money. Any time I have had some big goal, I've been able to stick to my budget without exception. Maybe you want to pay off your house or put your kids through college or spend two weeks at Disney World. Of course, those goals are just some examples—yours will probably be different. It doesn't even have to be a huge goal—if you feel overwhelmed by that, start out smaller. Perhaps it would be paying off a specific credit card, buying an extra month's worth of groceries, or saving up for next Christmas.

**Put your goal front and center.**

Whatever your specific goal is, focus on it with total dedication. Put photos that remind you of your goal on your fridge. Hang a picture beside your coffee maker. Wrap up your debit card with a piece of paper on which the goal is written. Make sure your goal is *everywhere* so that you are constantly reminded of it.

**Once you know where you're going, you need to make a map.**

Think of it as a road trip. Let's say you want to go from California to Virginia, like my youngest daughter and I did one year. You could just drive east, but then you run the risk of ending up in Maryland or North Carolina, depending where the roads take you. It makes more sense to navigate to your destination by using a map. Real life can be very similar to traveling a great distance.

An entrepreneurial trick is to create a map to your goal by working backward. Once you know your goal, it's fairly easy to work your way from the goal to the point you are at right now.

It looks something like this:

1.  The goal
2.  How much will it cost to reach the goal?
3.  When do you hope to reach the goal?
4.  How much do you need to put back per month to reach the goal in that time period?
5.  How much money is available to put toward your goal each month? Is it enough for your monthly goal?
6.  If not, what can you cut to acquire that amount of money? How can you make the extra money?

**Your mission, if you choose to accept it.**

So, what's your big goal? Create a map to get to it and give yourself some visual encouragement. This really works!

## Reaching Big Goals on a Little Budget

Frugalites typically fall into one of two categories (and there's often some crossover between these categories):

1.  Some of us are frugal by necessity. We have too much month and not enough money.

2. Some of us have Big Goals that should be far out of reach on our income, but we're determined to make them happen.

Both of these are exceptionally valid reasons to embrace frugality. Big Goals are the motivational carrot on the end of the thrifty stick that keep a lot of us going. I have personally achieved several Big Goals because of the fact that we are a frugal family. Daughter #1 had scholarships to college, and between those and my contributions, was able to get through and graduate without the student loans that cripple many young adults. Daughter #2 just finished trade school and we didn't take out debt for that either.

As a single mom, I was able to make enough money working online to support my kids and be home with them if we were super careful about our spending. I cherish the time I spent with them.

**Your Big Goals may be different.**

Perhaps you want to . . .

- Retire early while you're young enough to enjoy it
- Move someplace that you've always dreamed of living
- Travel the world
- Pay off all your debts, including your mortgage
- Give your kids a debt-free start in life
- Support a family member who can't support themselves, like an elderly parent
- Become a single-income household so one parent can be home with the kids

Some of these things may sound like they aren't in line with frugality, but that is the joy of thrift. You can make it anything you want. Your goals and dreams are yours and no one has any right to judge you for them as long as you can pay for it. This is your life, and if you have Big Goals, I say go for them!

**Here's how to reach a big goal.**

So, do you have a big goal? Are you wondering how to achieve it? Let me explain my process and maybe it will help you develop your own. I always seem to have some kind of big goal that I'm saving for and the next one really deserves an all-cap BIG. In fact, it probably sounds outright bat-crap crazy. Before I get into the meat of the goal, you should know that I had to bump it back by a year due to some massive medical bills. But that's okay because I had the money available to take care of what was needed. See how that works?

Anyhow, here it is. My wild confession.

Now that both of my babies are grown up and gainfully employed, I want to travel around the world for a year so I can dial back the amount of fourteen-hour days I've been working and enjoy a different lifestyle.

It's not going to be cheap to go on this adventure. In fact, it's going to cost a fair bit of money. But working toward this goal keeps me very motivated.

**I keep reminders of my goal everywhere.**
For example:

- I have a screensaver of an exotic locale that reminds me of where I want to be every time I turn on my laptop. Since that is one of the first things I do every morning, working online, I start my day with this goal in mind.
- I have pictures of different glimpses of faraway lands I plan to visit on the door of my fridge.
- This one is the most powerful. I printed off my dream itinerary and I keep it folded around my debit card. Talk about something that makes you think before spending!
- I have my suitcase in my room where it's always visible.
- I have a postcard of a destination tucked into the bathroom mirror.
- I get alerts from Airbnbs in the different cities I plan to visit sent to my email for even more reminders.

Every day, I am reminded of the big goal multiple times. It makes it far easier to resist the temptation of a temporary buzz from buying something I don't need.

Whatever your big goal is, do the same thing. Put it *everywhere*.

**Then, I have a special calendar.**
Any time I have ever had a big goal or some reason I have to make some extra money, I break it down on a calendar. The best way to reach a goal is to figure it out backward. So, start out like you're already there. Break this down into how much it costs to get there.

For me, the numbers look like this:

- Two months of expenses
- Airline tickets to the first destination
- The gear I intend to buy for my trip
- An emergency fund to help out with those miscellaneous expenses that are bound to occur when you are on the road

I have a total amount that I need to acquire over the next six months.

The other number you'll need is the amount of money you must have each month to pay all your current bills. Sadly, those bills don't go away just because you have a big goal. Here's how to break it down, step-by-step:

1. I multiplied the monthly budget by six, since I'll need it each month over the next six months.
2. Then, I added the two numbers together—my six-month budget and my big goal money.
3. That's the total I must earn over the next six months.
4. I divided by six to break it down into monthly amounts and wrote that amount on my calendar for each month over the next six.
5. Then, I divided the monthly amount by four to get a weekly total.
6. Then, I divided the weekly total by seven to get a daily total.
7. Now I know exactly what I have to make and put aside each month— each *day*—by some means to make my goal happen.

Will I actually earn the extra money every single day? Probably not. But there are things I can do to make up the shortfalls.

- I can sell things that I don't want to store.
- I can take on some freelance gigs.
- I can do some tasks myself that I'd normally pay someone to do, like cleaning the gutters.
- I can cut some money from my monthly expenses.

The whole time, I'll know exactly where I'm at and if I'm on track for making it happen. If for some reason I am not on track, I can push our departure date back a little or change the plan entirely.

There is nothing more powerful than breaking down a big goal day-by-day. If traveling around the world on a single mama budget sounds outrageous, you know what else sounds outrageous? Putting two kids through college on that same budget. Traveling around the country for a few months on that budget. Living a low-debt life on that budget. In fact, I've already begun and traveled through ten countries in six months.

### How will you reach your big goal?

If you want something badly enough, break it down like this and take a look. Is it possible in your time frame? Will you need to bring in extra money to do it? It seems ridiculously simple, but when you break down a big goal to its smallest parts, you are much more likely to achieve it.

# Part Three
# *Crisis Mode*

Have you ever had a sudden financial emergency? Maybe you lost your job. Maybe your car broke down and required an expensive repair. Maybe one of the family has had a medical emergency with large, out-of-pocket expenses. Whatever the reason, the steps you should take are basically the same.

**Begin a total spending freeze for a couple of days.**
One of the biggest mistakes people make when faced with a shocking expense is to go on spending as though they still have the same budget. Perhaps they go and buy something to try and make themselves feel better. Maybe they just continue spending like they always did, with hundreds of dollars going out for kids' activities, dinners out, and shopping trips.

Just stop. You need a few days to reassess your budget and see where you're at. You don't want to regret the expenditures you make right after a financial catastrophe. Put yourself on a complete spending freeze for the next few days while you evaluate the change in your financial situation.

**Don't sign anything right away.**
This is especially true if you've lost your job. As much loyalty as you may have had to your company, they clearly don't feel the same sense of loyalty toward you. Many companies will try to get you to sign paperwork right away to "settle the details." Trust me when I say, these details will be skewed in their favor—not yours. You do *not* have to sign anything while sitting there, stunned at your sudden change in circumstances. It's vital that you take the time to read over everything carefully. Your severance package, your 401K, any accrued pension, and unemployment benefits will be at risk. In some cases, you can negotiate this, even though you are not sitting in the power seat. Don't commit

to any type of agreement while you're reeling, particularly if they try to coerce you into signing immediately. Regardless of what you may be told, any delay in your unemployment benefits or severance will be minimal.

The same goes for an outrageous repair bill or other unexpected expense. Give yourself time to think things over and perhaps seek a second opinion before agreeing to spend thousands of dollars. Obviously, with some medical issues, time is of the essence and you may not be able to mull over decisions for several days.

### Create a budget for necessities.

You already know your bottom line, right? We talked about it in the redefining necessities section on page 10. It's absolutely vital that you drop your expenditures to the bare minimum until you are able to get another stream of income. You need to take a look at where your money goes and base your new budget on the necessities. Although having a vehicle in each stall of the garage and an iPhone in the hand of every family member is nice, these are not necessary to sustaining life.

### Slash luxury spending.

Reduce your monthly payments by cutting frivolous expenses. Look at every single monthly payment that comes out of your bank account and slash relentlessly. Consider cutting the following:

- Cable
- Cell phones
- Home phones
- Gym memberships
- Restaurant meals
- Unnecessary driving
- Entertainment such as trips to the movies, the skating rink, or the mall

It may not be a lot of fun, but it's absolutely necessary until your crisis is under control.

### Start looking for new streams of income.

You know those people who tell you that it's easy to find a new job if you wouldn't be such a snob? Ignore them. The job market of today is not the job market of a decade ago. Jobs are few and far between, and good jobs are as elusive as unicorns in Central Park. You may need to look at creating your own streams of income, like:

- Creating an online business.
- Using your expertise from your job (or former job) to work as a consultant.
- Doing various small jobs.
- Creating a home-based business with a low start-up cost (now's not the time to make a large investment).
- Using creative skills to make things to sell.
- Providing a service. Maybe you can cook, sew, repair things, or build things. Lots of people can't and will be willing to pay someone who can.

The more streams of income you can create, the more financially stable you'll become.

### Sell stuff.

All that stuff you've been meaning to go through in the basement just might be the key to keeping a roof over your head. It's time to have a yard sale, start an eBay account, or get on Craigslist (both free at the time of publication) and start selling things that have just been sitting there for a while. Your trash might be another person's treasure. Instead of regifting those things in your attic, sell them so they can become someone else's clutter. You'll be surprised how much money you can make while decluttering your home.

### Sometimes there's a silver lining.

Of course, every situation is different but if you look for the upside, it can make things a whole lot more tolerable. Take job loss, for example. Although sudden unemployment can be terrifying, it can also be the start of something wonderful. When I lost my job in the automotive industry, I was devastated. As a single mom, how was I going to continue taking care of my two girls with no income?

Instead of being a bad thing, it turned out to be the best thing that ever happened to me. I was able to take the writing I'd been dabbling in for years from a hobby to a full-time job. I made a conscious decision *not* to search for another job, but to follow my dream of being a writer and editor. Maybe I succeeded because it was do-or-die time. There was no option but to make it work. I began writing for other websites, started my own site, and began outlining books. As it turned out, that shocking, unceremonious discussion in the automotive manager's office was the best thing that ever happened to me. I've read many success stories that began the same way. Sometimes what seems like an ending can actually be a new beginning.

A health crisis may not seem like a positive, but if it encourages a loved one to turn over a new leaf and live a healthier lifestyle or improves their current situation it can have some positive benefits. If your car breaks down—well, not everything can be painted in a positive light. But your attitude is everything. If you can manage to keep your sense of humor and your positivity intact, you'll survive much more easily than someone who crumbles at the first sign of a financial emergency.

## How to Raise Money Fast When Things Go Wrong

Have you ever been in a situation where you need to make money fast? There are two ways to go about this quickly. Sell stuff or sell services. The things you sell will usually fall into a couple of categories. They're either things you have that you no longer want (or are willing to part with) or they are things that you make.

- Have a yard sale
- List unwanted items on Craigslist or local online marketplaces
- Recommend items on which you get a commission
- Sell handmade goods at craft sales, by word of mouth, or at festivals and fairs (the last one requires some investment and may not be good for a "need money fast" situation)
- Take gold or silver jewelry to a place that will purchase it by weight
- Take unwanted clothing to a store that will sell it on a consignment basis (this also works well if you have children who have good-quality clothing that has been outgrown)
- Sell things on Etsy or eBay
- Take electronics or other expensive items to a pawn shop (you won't get the most money at a pawn shop, but you'll get immediate money)
- Sell excess garden goodies from a stand in your front yard
- If you have a really good eye, you can make money buying cool vintage stuff at yard sales and online, cleaning it up, then reselling

it to an antique shop (be careful though—you can just as easily lose money doing this)

Some of us have specialized skills that make selling services easier—for example, I am a writer and editor, so I focus my money-earning on those two skills. You might be particularly handy, so you could focus your skills on doing home repairs. Perhaps you are great at sewing and can take on alterations and mending jobs. But it isn't necessary to have a skill set to bring in another stream of income. You simply have to be willing to do small jobs that may or may not be short term. Here are some ideas to get you started. This list, of course, is by no means comprehensive.

- Cleaning houses
- Cleaning out vacated rental properties (as a perk, sometimes you get to keep items that have been abandoned, and you can sell them on Craigslist or make use of them yourself)
- Yardwork: raking, mowing, etc.
- Landscaping
- Trimming trees
- Cleaning out gutters
- Repairing items: home repairs, small appliance repairs—whatever you're good at fixing, there is likely a person who needs that item fixed
- Cooking for those too busy to cook for themselves
- Babysitting
- Before and after school childcare (It can be really tough for working parents to find someone willing to drive their children to school and pick them up)
- Weekend or overnight childcare
- Pet-sitting
- Dog-walking
- Laundry service (I recommend doing this at a laundromat instead of running up your own utility bills—you can build the price of the coin operated machines into your fee)
- Run errands—some folks are working during regular business hours and don't have the time to do those little errands like stopping by the dry cleaner, going to the grocery store, etc.
- Shovel snow

- Help people move—if you have a strong back, you can be the hired muscle
- Wash cars
- Do a paper route (it's not just for kids anymore)
- Recycle aluminum or plastic
- Recycle scrap metal—if you have a truck, run an ad offering to pick up used appliances, etc. (most people are thrilled to have someone haul off their old junk)
- Haul away trash—this is another use for your truck
- Do farm chores
- Pick up poop—an old friend I used to know made a *lot* of money from his willingness to pick up dog poop in people's backyard on a weekly basis
- Rent out a room in your home—you can get big dollars if you live near a college
- If you sew, you can make money doing mending and alterations—many tailors charge up to $20 to hem a pair of pants

**Here are a few keys to success.**
It's important to make a good impression on your customers. Handle these small jobs just like you would a corporate job and follow these key steps.

- Be professional
- Arrive promptly
- Be courteous—the customer is always right
- Be tidy in your appearance
- Work hard
- Try to exceed the person's expectations

Keep these principles in mind and you will never be lacking jobs. Word of mouth is the very best form of advertising.

**Get the word out.**
Sometimes you can find work through people you know—maybe they expressed a need to have someone walk Fido partway through the day. Other times, you will need to search a little harder to find customers for your services.

- Put an ad on Craigslist
- Find some local message boards online and post your services there
- Make flyers and hand them out in your neighborhood (be sure to respect the wishes of those homes that say "no flyers")
- Post flyers on telephone poles if that is allowed in your area
- Put a sign in your front yard—I used to advertise "daycare space available" at my home
- Put an ad in the classified section of your local paper
- Put a sign up on grocery store or other community bulletin boards

Remember, this doesn't have to be something you do for the long-term. (Although, if you begin doing something like daycare, you need to be reliable unless it was initially agreed on that it would be a short-term gig.) If you're willing to get out there and be productive, you can often solve or at least ease your financial problems quickly.

## When It Rains Money Problems, It Pours

Have you ever noticed that, financially speaking, when it rains, it pours? For example, when times are tight, you are more likely to bounce a payment from the bank. The bank is quick to attack with fees that drain your account even further, making it likely that more things will bounce, and more fees will be added. Or when you have a big medical bill, you also end up taking time off work, which means you have less money to tackle that enormous bill.

If you've ever looked at my website, TheOrganicPrepper.com, you know that I think about big things like pandemics, nuclear war, and riots in the streets. But I know (from painful experience) that personal things can cause a lot of upheaval when you are on a tight budget. And if Murphy's Law holds true (and it often does), whatever can go wrong, will go wrong, generally at the worst possible time.

Despite this, you can take those challenges and learn from them. While you're wrestling them into submission, you can use this chance to find a bright side. Here's one example from a financial catastrophe I ran into a few years ago. (And lest you immediately shut this book and return it to the place where you purchased it, remember that I've managed to raise two girls on a single mom budget *and* put them through college without debt. It's just that life in general these days is fraught with financial pitfalls we must leap over or climb out from. It would be disingenuous to pretend that once I became frugal, I never had money problems again.) I was driving down the road one day when I noticed that my car was beginning to overheat. I pulled over, let it cool down, and limped in at twenty miles an hour to a nearby shop, hoping it was something little like a leaky radiator cap. Alas, it was something big like leaky head gaskets. And by big, I mean about $2,000. Oh, and another week or so without a vehicle.

My poor little emergency fund, that I had been cultivating and growing, was immediately kaput, along with a couple of weeks of pay. Imagine my delight. I had the only Honda in a make known for reliability to blow a head gasket. I was seriously upset. In a funk. Blue as the moon. Which, of course, would get me precisely nowhere.

**First, improve your attitude.**
I decided to wax philosophical and find the bright side. If I allowed myself to linger in that funk, all I would do is think about what I was missing, how I was stuck at home, and how awful things are. *Wah.* Not productive.

I started feeling ever-so-slightly better when I thought to myself, *Hey, this is practice for a real, genuine, can't-leave-the-house disaster. I can write about this.* Not much better, but better enough that I was not weeping into my coffee or planning a dramatic ten-mile walk to the nearest Starbucks so that I could plunge face first into a gigantic Frappuccino for solace. Then I started thinking about the stuff that I had really planned on getting at the store to which I'd been headed when my SUV dramatically gave up its grip on drivability. Like laundry detergent, for example. I had also planned to hit the farmers' market and pick up some veggies that I wanted. Then I started thinking about the awesome ways I could deal with these things. And I felt inspired and energized because of the challenges. Also, I had something interesting to write about, because many of us are in a situation very much like this, where one large unexpected expense can be life-altering . . . at least temporarily.

While it still bites the big one that I had to spend $2,000 on a vehicle repair (on a flippin' *Honda*, no less), as soon as I changed my attitude and began thinking about solutions instead of problems, I felt a thousand times better and reverted to my normal optimistic self. As Einstein said, "Everything is energy and that's all there is to it. Match the frequency of the reality you want, and you cannot help but to get that reality. It can be no other way. This is not philosophy. This is physics."

**Second, be creative in your solutions.**

In response to the instant "Oh my gosh, I'm stranded, and I need so much stuff from the store" reaction, I began doing an inventory of what I had on hand to fulfill those needs. I'd been planning to make my own laundry detergent for ages and had all of the supplies on hand in such abundance that I could have washed clothes from now until the Second Coming and still have homemade laundry soap left over for those white robes.

As far as the food goes, well, wants aren't needs. We had, as always, a stockpile in the pantry, home canned goods, and stuff in the freezer. We honestly would have been perfectly well fed if we didn't go to the store or farmers' market for the next six months. It might have gotten a bit repetitious, but we'd have been nourished and far from hungry. Plus, I always have vast amounts of coffee on hand, so that I'll be pleasant throughout whatever Armageddon might strike.

I realized that there wasn't one single thing I desperately needed that I couldn't make or improvise. And maybe I'm weird but I find improvisation to be a lot of fun, and I get an actual rush when my makeshift solutions end up working really well. I really like that quote "necessity is the mother of invention" far better than the Murphy quote.

**Third, there are usually some silver linings.**

We had moved recently when our vehicle gave that sickening gasp, and now that we were on foot, my daughter and I decided to take a different route and go for a walk each day to explore our new area. This was some great mom/kid time, good exercise, and we were able to learn more about our surroundings instead of always being too busy to go exploring. In many personal catastrophes, there are similar perks if you look at them the right way.

- A loss of a job means you have more time to spend with your family.
- A financial crunch means that you might spend more time cooking wholesome ingredients from scratch instead of buying fast food or convenience items.
- Not having a vehicle means you save money because you have no place to spend money.
- If you have more time on your hands, no matter what the reason, you can get going on some of those projects you've been putting off.
- When you need something that you can't afford to pay for, sometimes you can learn a new skill and create it yourself.

- If the power goes out, the family comes together. There are no video games or TV shows or Internet-surfing sessions to get in the way of hanging out. Memories are made of times like these.

Sometimes I'm astounded at the solutions my kids come up with. They are so bright and creative, and those talents really shine in situations where problem solving is necessary.

**Challenges build character.**

By learning to turn a negative situation into a more positive experience, we become stronger and more adaptable. That's what survival is all about. The most well-read person on the planet will have difficulty adapting to troublesome times if they've never had to do so. How you react to those bad things that happen is the true definition of the person you are. Personally, I choose happiness and optimism. The rain always stops falling eventually. And then the flowers can grow.

> "When we long for life without difficulties, remind us that oaks grow strong in contrary winds and diamonds are made under pressure."
> —Peter Marshall

## Dealing with Emotional Spending

Emotional spending gets the best of many a frugality fan.

- Are you happy? Go buy something to make a good day even better.
- Are you sad? Go buy something to cheer yourself up.
- Are you having a rough day? Go buy something because, darn it, you deserve it.
- Are you angry? Go buy something to distract you from your rage.
- Did you just accomplish a goal? Go buy something to celebrate.

Does this sound familiar? If it does, you may be an emotional spender. And if you are, you're not alone. Half of Americans surveyed in 2017[1] admit-

---

1    Erin El Issa, "Americans Are Emotionally Overspending," Marketwatch, Mar. 3, 2017, https://www.marketwatch.com/story/americans-are-emotionally-over spending-2017-02-27

ted to emotional spending, and many of them said it led them into deeper credit card debt.

Want some tips that can help you get a handle on emotional spending? If buying things is your go-to mechanism for dealing with your emotions, how do you *stop*? The following ideas can help.

**Come up with some no-spend rewards for yourself.**
This could be one-on-one time with a loved one or close friend, a long hike on a Saturday afternoon, a trip to the park with your children, visiting the museum on free admission day, a visit to the animal shelter to pet the dogs (this can be dangerous if you're anything like me!), a trip to the library for some good books, or performing volunteer work that makes your heart feel full. I like to sit down and watch a movie on Netflix or Amazon Prime as a reward after a long day.

**Put the kibosh on impulse spending.**
This isn't easy, but you're going to have to delay your gratification for a while. When you see something that you weren't planning to buy, and you suddenly want it like crazy . . . *stop*. Stopping doesn't mean you'll never get it. It means that you're going to think it through and make sure you truly want it. Give yourself twenty-four hours to think it over. Will it harm your budget? Will it cost you even more money to maintain the item? Will you be paying it off for years? Make your spending choices very consciously and not impulsively.

**Unsubscribe.**
Does your inbox look like mine? Is it full of newsletters from retailers who breathlessly announce "the best sale ever" on a daily basis? It's hard to say no to those all the time. Think about it—they're written by marketers who spend years learning how to part you from your money.

Unsubscribe. Yes, you'll probably miss out on some deals, but if you need to go to a store, you can usually find the same deals available in store or available to download online. Trust me, you don't need the constant barrage of temptation. I recently unsubscribed from 98, count 'em, 98 retail email lists. What a relief! We'll talk more about this later in the book.

**Avoid places that make you want to spend money.**
For me, it's HomeGoods and Target. I simply cannot walk into those stores and walk out with nothing. It's all so pretty, so unique, so

must-have-this-in-my-life that I rarely escape unscathed. So, I just don't go there. If I *do* go, it is with cash that I have put aside for this specific purpose. I leave my debit card at home and that way I can't be tempted to purchase things that are over my budget. Your own can't-resist store may be different—it may be the whole mall—but whatever it is, you can't spend money there if you don't go.

### Don't save your credit card on online stores.

This is a hard-learned lesson from Amazon. The added step of putting in my card each time keeps me from just hitting one-click purchase and ending up with a lot of frivolous things in my mailbox. Amazon can be the source of many great purchases, but it can also be the biggest expense on your credit card bill.

### Kick cable TV to the curb.

I've used streaming services like Netflix for so long that I'd completely forgotten what it was like to see the barrage of commercials until I visited a family member who has cable. Every ten minutes, three or four commercials were urging me to spend money, buy fast food, or save the dogs in a NYC shelter. Why put yourself through that?

### Block ads online.

Of course, the Internet brings commercials right to you through all sorts of nefarious methods, like cookies from websites you've visited. Try AdBlock or some other method to keep those ads from flashing before your eyes on every website you visit. Heck, even email services like Yahoo have ads on the sidebar based on your Internet habits.

### Figure out what's going on in your head.

If you've been overspending recently or feeling out of control with regard to money, what is going on in your life that is making you feel this way? Introspection isn't often fun, but it can be necessary. When you pinpoint the real problem, then you need to search for a solution to it (assuming there is one—that isn't possible in every case). If a solution isn't possible, then you need to plan for best- and worst-case scenarios. Personally, I always feel better when there's a plan.

**You must create new habits.**

If emotional spending has always been your go-to response, it will take some time to create the new habits that you desire. But it can absolutely be done.

- Know your triggers.
- Have fiscally responsible substitutes ready.
- Practice, practice, practice.
- Don't beat yourself up too much if you backslide—we're only human!

You've got this!

## What to Do If You Truly Can't Pay Your Bills

Let's get into *real* crisis mode here. Let's talk about poverty. I don't mean the kind you're talking about when your friends invite you to go shopping or for a night out and you say, "No, I can't. I'm poor right now." I don't mean the situation when you'd like to get a nicer car but decide you should just stick to the one you have because you don't have a few thousand for a down payment. I don't mean the scene at the grocery store when you decide to get ground beef instead of steak.

I'm talking about when you have already done the weird mismatched meals from your pantry that are made up of cooked rice, stale crackers, and a can of peaches, and you've moved on to wondering what on earth you're going to feed your kids. Or when you get an eviction notice for non-payment of rent, a shut-off notice for your utilities, and a repo notice for your car and there's absolutely nothing you can do about any of those notices because there *is no money.*

If you've never been this level of broke, I'm very glad. I *have* been this broke. I know that it is soul-destroying when no matter how hard you work, how many part-time jobs you squeeze in, and how much you cut, you simply don't make enough money to survive in the world today. Being part of the working poor is incredibly frustrating and discouraging. It is a sickening feeling when you're just barely hanging in there and suddenly, an unexpected expense crops up and decimates your tight budget. Maybe your child gets sick and needs a trip to the doctor and some medicine. Perhaps a family member is involved in an accident and can't work for a few weeks. It could be that your car breaks down and you need it to get back-and-forth to work because you live too far out in the country for public transit.

As our economy continues to crumble, these are the situations going on in more homes across the country every single day. It's simple to believe that the people suffering like this are just lazy, or not trying, or are spending frivolously. No one wants to think that these things can occur through no fault of the individual. Why? Because that means these things could also happen to them.

Every time I write on my blog about crushing poverty, someone in the comments section replies with a smug declaration about how people need to get an education, hang on to a job, buy cheaper food . . . there's a litany of condescending advice. It's absolutely horrible, the lack of compassion you will see, and if you're in the situation I'm describing, you need to try to let the criticism roll off of you.

The advice I have may be controversial to those who haven't been there, but let's talk about prioritizing your payments when you can't pay your bills. I'm not promoting irresponsibility here. It's just math. **When you have less money coming in than you have obligated to go out, you will not be able to pay all of your bills.** It's that simple.

First, do a quick audit of your financial situation so you can see where you're at. This list of priorities assumes that you have some money coming in, but not enough to meet your obligations. When things improve, you can try to catch up, but for now, you simply have to choose survival. I suggest the following order of payments.

### 1. Pay for shelter first

Your number one priority is keeping a roof over your head. That roof may not be the roof of the house you are in now, though, if your circumstances have changed and you can no longer afford it. If you can still manage to pay your rent/mortgage, do so in order to keep your family housed. If you rent, and your rent is a reasonable price, make this the first payment you make from your limited funds. You really, truly don't want to be homeless, and moving is expensive. Try your best to stay put. If you own, consider your property taxes and insurance as part of your mortgage, because if you stop paying any of these, your home will be foreclosed on.

If you can't pay your mortgage, property taxes, and insurance, you have a while before the home gets foreclosed on and you are forced to move out. If this is the case, it's essential that you put aside money for the place where you'll move should you have to leave your home. You're going to need first and last months' rent and deposits in many cases, particularly since your credit isn't going to be stellar due to your financial situation. When you are in this situation, it can be difficult to force yourself to save money when so many things are being left unpaid, but if you ever hope to bail yourself out of this situation, you absolutely must do this.

The laws vary from state to state[2], but basically, this is the timeline:

- When you make the decision to let your house go back to the lender, you will have a month or two before they send you a notice of default.
- From that point, you usually have three months before the foreclosure proceedings begin. During those three months, you should be saving the money you would normally be putting toward your mortgage.
- At some point, you'll get a notice to vacate the premises.
- When this happens, you have two options. You can choose to move to a different home, or you can file for bankruptcy, if you feel your situation is such that there is absolutely no way out.
- If you file for bankruptcy, the home can't be resold by the lender for three more months, giving you more time to put aside money for your move.

Should we all pay the bills that we have promised to pay? Of course we should. Our word is very important. Remember, though, that the information here is for people who are in a position in which they *do not have the money to pay*. So, the bottom line is this: either pay your housing costs or put aside money for future housing as your first expenditure.

## 2. Buy food

You have to eat, and so do your children. If you don't eat, you'll get sick, and then your situation will be even more dire.

- Stick to simple, wholesome basics and cook from scratch. Beans and rice have fed many a family.
- Tap into your inner southerner and make inexpensive, filling meals like biscuits and gravy.

---

2   Amy Loftsgordon, "Summary of State Foreclosure Laws," NOLO, accessed on June 29, 2020, https://www.nolo.com/legal-encyclopedia/free-books/foreclosure-book/chapter11-1.html

- Make soup to stretch just a few ingredients to feed a family.
- Save *all* of your leftovers, even the ones on people's plates. Add them to a container in the freezer and make a soup from that at the end of the week.
- Clean up after the potluck at church. Sometimes you can take home the leftovers.
- Don't skip meals to stretch your food further. You need your health and your strength to overcome this situation.
- Go to the library and check out a book on local edibles. Go foraging in the park or in nearby wooded areas.
- See if your grocery store sells out-of-date produce for use for animals. There's often a fair bit you can salvage and add to soups or casseroles. (This is the only way we were able to have vegetables and meat during one particularly painful stretch when my oldest daughter was young.)

In a worst-case scenario, food banks are an option as well.

### 3. Pay for essential utilities

You should be cutting your utility usage to the bare minimum and using every trick in the book to keep your bills as low as possible. If your utilities get shut off, it's going to be difficult to cook from scratch and you won't be able to keep leftovers from spoiling. You need the water running from your taps to drink, cook with, and clean. Depending on the climate and the season, heat may be vital as well. If you can't pay the entire bill, call the utility companies and try to make payment arrangements. If your utilities are shut off, then you will have a hefty reconnection fee on top of the bill.

Another point to remember is that our culture believes it's absolutely necessary that all homes be plugged in to the utility system. If you have a work-around, like wood heat and hand-pumped well water, and decide that your utilities are not essential, you need to be prepared to face those whose opinions differ. Some cities have condemned homes which are not connected to the grid,[3] and if you have children who are of school age, know that "concerned" teachers and neighbors have been known to report such situations to

---

3  "Court Rules Off-the-Grid Living Is Illegal," Off-the-Grid News, Feb. 22, 2014, https://www.offthegridnews.com/current-events/court-rules-off-the-grid -living-is-illegal/

the child welfare authorities. (Recently an off-grid homeschooling family had their children removed from the home by police.[4])

### 4. Pay for car/work necessities

What must you have in order to keep working? For me, it's the Internet, since I work online. All of my clients contact me via email and the work I do requires that I be able to send it to them and research things online. I live in the country, so driving to the library on a daily basis would cost more than my monthly Internet fees. For another person, this necessity might be the cost of public transit or keeping their vehicle on the road so that they can get to work. Choose the least expensive options to keep yourself working, but maintain your job-related necessities.

### 5. Pay for anything else

After you've paid all of the above, if you have money left over, now is the time to pay your other expenses. These expenses include debt that you've incurred, contracts you are involved in (like cell phone plans, etc.). Choose very carefully how you dole out any remaining money.

- Keep one phone going, with the lowest possible payment. This is necessary for work, for your children or their school to contact you in the event of an emergency, and as a contact point for your financial situation. Compare the cost of a cell phone, landline, or VOIP phone. Every family member does not require a phone—you just need one. (I actually did go for a couple of years with no phone at all, but I'm uniquely antisocial and had email by which I could be reached.)
- If it's at all possible, try to use the snowball method made famous by Dave Ramsey (more on that on page 30) to pay off your debts and bail yourself out of your situation. Being free from debt will allow you to live a much freer life in the future.
- If paying off debt is not possible, try to make the minimum payments.
- If the minimum payments are not possible, you may have to default, at least temporarily, on debts.

---

4   Adriana Velez, "Police Seize 10 Children from Off-the-Grid, 'Unschooling' Family," The Stir - Cafe Mom, May 8, 2015, https://thestir.cafemom.com/bizarre _news/185732/police_seize_10_children_from

- Buy some pantry staples. If you can add some extra rice or cans of tomatoes to the pantry, it will help see you through this tight situation.
- Be relentless in deciding what will be paid and what will not. This is not the time for arguments like "But it's our only form of entertainment" or "We deserve this one luxury." Cut all non-essentials until things improve.
- Focus on the most frugal options possible.

**Things will get better.**

I've been down this road. I really get it. It saddens me to see people I love in this situation now. If you are in a situation in which you can't pay your bills, I'm sorry.

I'm sorry about . . .

- The embarrassment you feel when you can't afford to meet someone for coffee.
- The sick feeling of seeing the bills pile up on the counter and not being able to do anything about it.
- The knot in your stomach every time the phone rings and it's a 1-800 number that you *know* is a bill collector.
- The stress of knowing you can't remain in your home.
- The fear that someone will say you aren't taking care of your kids and they'll be taken away.
- The humiliation when people don't understand and think it's all your fault.
- The hopelessness of watching the bank account empty out the day your pay goes in, and still having a dozen things unpaid.
- The overwhelming discouragement of having fees tacked on to debts you already can't pay.
- The anxiety over what tomorrow will bring.

It will get better. You'll find a way to make it work. You just have to survive while you make it happen. Maybe you will pool your resources with another family, or get a raise, or find a cheaper place. But you *will* find a way. Life may not be exactly as it was before, but it will be good again.

# Part Four
# Home Cheap Home

Although we've talked about all sorts of things outside the home, true frugality starts within the home. The price of your housing and utilities are necessities and keeping your necessities as low as possible is the key to decreasing the amount of money you spend every month. In this section, we'll go through some ideas for keeping these expenses low. We'll start off easy and then build up to a potentially radical solution.

## Utilities

Even when times aren't exceptionally tight, it pays off to keep a close eye on your utility usage. In this section, we'll discuss some tips for keeping them as low as possible.

### Save on electricity.

Aside from staying warm and cold, there are many ways to cut your electric bill that won't lead to candlelight and deprivation. You may have heard of some of these before, but a little refresher never hurt anybody.

- **Turn the lights off when you leave a room.** It might be worth putting a motion-sensitive switch in frequently visited rooms like bathrooms and hallways, especially if you have children (or careless adults) in your home. You can find these at any hardware store and they're so easy to install that even I have managed it without electrocuting myself.
- **Use natural light.** During the day, there's no reason to have a lamp on in your home unless it's incredibly overcast. Open up the curtains and let the sun light your way for free.

- **Unplug electricity-sucking appliances when you're done with them.** Televisions, coffee makers, treadmills, office equipment, computers, and chargers (even when they aren't being used) are called "energy vampires" and they can suck up many kilowatts of power over the course of a month. For the sake of ease, consider a power strip in each room so you can turn off multiple energy-drainers at a time with the flip of a switch.

- **Be strategic with your thermostat.** Another good investment is a thermostat you can set to be lower when nobody is home during the day and higher in the mornings when it's chilly.

- **Keep your fridge and freezer at their ideal temperatures for maximum efficiency.** For refrigerators, that's 35°F to 37°F and for freezers, that's 0°F.

- **Change your bulbs to compact fluorescents.** Each one can save you $50 in electricity of the lifespan of the bulb.

- **Use the crockpot or microwave instead of the oven.** The crockpot uses far less power than heating up the oven (and also your house). For reheating, if you use a microwave, it can save many kilowatts of power over reheating food in the oven or on the stovetop.

- **Use less hot water.** Wash clothing in cold water. Only run washing machines and dishwashers when they're full. Take shorter showers and turn the water off while shaving or shampooing.

- **Hang your clothes to dry.** This can save a lot of money, as dryers consume a lot of energy. And in the summer, you'll save even more because your air conditioner won't have to combat the heat of the dryer.

- **Get an energy audit**. Your local electric company may offer an energy audit for free. This can really help you see where you're using power you may not actually need.

**Save on water.**

Here are a few suggestions for reducing the amount of water you use on a daily basis. This list is by no means comprehensive, and not all of these solutions will work for everyone's situation. First, take notes from those who live without running water. Just think: If you had to physically acquire every drop of water used in your home, whether by pumping it from a well or lugging it from a water source, you'd already be taking many of these lower-tech steps.

- **Reuse cooking water.** If you have boiled pasta or vegetables, use this water for making soup. You will have retained some of the nutrients and flavor from the first thing you cooked in the water.
- **Landscape with plants that grow naturally in your area.** They should require little in the way of additional watering.
- **Grow organic.** Chemical fertilizers can increase a plant's need for water.
- **Shave with less water.** When shaving, rinse your razor in a cup instead of under running water.
- **Skip the dishwasher.** Doing the dishes by hand uses far less water.
- **Set up a rinse basin.** Instead of running water over each dish to rinse, fill one side of the sink or a basin with rinse water containing a splash of white vinegar. Running water uses up to four gallons per minute.
- **Use a glass of water to brush your teeth.** Try this instead of running the tap the entire time.
- **Mulch.** Use an organic mulch in your garden to help retain moisture.
- **Use that basin again.** Wash produce in a basin of water instead of under running water.
- **You can even reuse aquarium water.** When you clean out your fish tank, reserve the water for your garden. Your veggies will love the nutrient boost!
- **Get rain barrels.** Harvest rainwater for your garden.
- **Use less water per flush.** Use a brick, a filled plastic bottle, or a float booster to fill space in the back of the toilet tank. This reduces the amount of water used in each flush.
- **Do you have to flush every time?** Speaking of flushing, you may have heard the rhyme, "If it's yellow, let it mellow. If it's brown, flush it down."
- **Use your gray water.** Devise a gray water catchment system for your shower, your washing machine, and your kitchen. This water can be used for flushing, watering plants, and for cleaning.
- **Take shorter showers.** Try to reduce them to five minutes— this can save up to 1,000 gallons per month! If you can't handle a five-minute shower, every two minutes you shorten your shower time by can save approximately 150 to 200 gallons per month.
- **Update your shower head.** It's quick and relatively inexpensive to install a water-saving shower head.

- **When you have a shower, plug the tub.** Use the water you collect for handwashing laundry.
- **Wash some clothing by hand.** It will use far less water than your washing machine. Be sure to save the water for other uses.
- **Only run your dishwasher if it's full.** If you do use a dishwasher, run it only when it's completely full—this can save you 1,000 gallons per month.
- **Don't waste what you drop.** If you drop a tray of ice cubes, pop them into a pet dish or into your potted plants.
- **Use a basin in the bathroom, too.** When washing your hands, dip them in a basin of water, lather up, then rinse under running water. Running water uses up to four gallons per minute.
- **Upgrade your faucets.** Update them with inexpensive aerators with flow restrictors.
- **Use a nozzle on your hose.** This way, you are only putting water where you want it, not spraying it uselessly as you walk to the garden.
- **Repair leaks.** At the rate of one drip per second, that adds up to five gallons per day . . . literally down the drain.
- **Research purchases of new appliances.** If you are buying new items for your home, opt for those which use water more efficiently, like front-loading washing machines and low-flush toilets.

## How to Make Cleaning Products That Won't Kill You

One of my favorite parts of spring is scrubbing down the entire house, throwing open the windows so the breeze can come through, and hanging rugs and bedding outside. Maybe it's weird but I just love spring cleaning. However, what I don't love is the expensive, chemical-laden cleaning products from the store. That's why I spend just a teeny bit of time making my own, from simple, non-toxic ingredients.

We're living in a toxic civilization that seems sparkling clean and sanitary but is actually poisoning us. Many of the chemicals that we are exposed to on a daily basis never leave our bodies but accumulate in fat and bone marrow. There's little oversight and testing on those chemicals. Cleaning products are rife with corrosive substances, irritating artificial fragrances, and petrochemicals. They can cause immediate symptoms like skin irritation, respiratory issues, allergic reactions, and eye irritation. Even worse, they can cause long-term issues like hormone disruption, brain cell death, permanent lung damage, and cancer.

**It's quick, frugal, and easy to make non-toxic cleaning products.**
That's why I spend just a few moments of extra time making my own cleaning
products, from simple, non-toxic ingredients. I order most of my basic supplies online in bulk and keep them on hand, so I can always whip them up as
needed. Not only are you sparing your health, but you'll save a lot of money
with DIY products!

Here's what you need for a clean home:

- Baking soda
- Borax
- Vinegar
- Essential oils in your favorite scents
- Liquid castile soap in your favorite scent
- Non-smelly cooking oil (I get something inexpensive for this, since
  we won't be consuming it)

You can make everything you need from those items.

**Scouring powder:**
- 1 part baking soda
- 1 part borax
- 10–20 drops essential oil of choice

In a mason jar, mix the baking soda with the borax. Sprinkle in some
essential oil. (I like citrus or mint smells for the fresh clean fragrance.)
Combine the mixture well and put it in a sunny windowsill for a week to let
the powders absorb the scent of the oils. If you aren't concerned about the
fragrance you can use this right away.

**Spray surface cleaner #1:**
- 2 parts white vinegar
- 1 part water
- 5–10 drops essential oil of choice

Fill a spray bottle with white vinegar and water. Add your favorite essential oils to cover the vinegar smell. This works on non-wood surfaces and
glass.

**Spray surface cleaner #2:**

This one is good for wood surfaces. Mix this up as you go along, because the oil can become rancid.

- 3 parts unscented cooking oil
- 1 part vinegar
- 5–10 drops essential oil of choice

Yes, basically, it's salad dressing. I like to add sandalwood essential oil to this because it's . . . well, woody, but lots of folks use citrus oil to get that lemon fresh fragrance. Spray this on wooden furniture and work with the grain.

**Hardwood floor cleaner:**

Your hardwoods will gleam with this cleaner. Note: this cleaner is only for real wood floors. If you use it on laminate it will be slippery.

- 16 parts hot water
- 1 part cooking oil
- ½ part lemon or lime juice
- 5–10 drops citrus essential oil

**Another floor cleaner:**
- 16 parts hot water
- 1 part borax
- ½ part castile soap
- A few drops tea tree essential oil
- A few drops other essential oil for fragrance

If your floor is particularly greasy you can replace half of the water with white vinegar.

**Drain cleaner:**

This DIY was provided by a reader, Mimi.

- ¼ cup baking soda
- ¼ cup salt
- ¼ cup cream of tartar

Mix the ingredients together, then sprinkle into the affected drain. Follow with 2 cups of boiling water, and then let it sit for one hour. Rinse, and your drain will be clear.

**Laundry detergent:**
There are lots of great things about making your own laundry detergent. It's very frugal. The ingredients don't cost much at all to make a gigantic batch. I checked online so that my prices were accurate, but I believe some of these items can be purchased locally at a lower price. You can usually find all or most of the ingredients at Walmart. It costs about $20 for a huge tub of laundry soap—about twenty pounds of detergent. Since you'll only be using one to three tablespoons per load, the amount you can make for $20 will probably last for about 250 loads—about 8 cents per load of laundry.

It's incredibly easy. The thing that took the longest was chopping up the soap. If you had to use a hand grater for the soap, you might want to sit down at the table and turn something interesting on Netflix, because that would definitely take a while. I used the dry container for my Vitamix, and it took about 10 to 15 minutes to chop up all of the soap. Aside from that, it was a matter of tearing the boxes of the individual ingredients open, dumping them into a tub, and stirring.

If you have a family member with sensitive skin or allergies, you can easily adjust this recipe. Several recipes I found online did not contain the OxiClean, for example. You could also choose different soap such as Ivory or castile. Whatever your needs, when you make the item yourself, you can switch things around until it is perfect for your family.

This is what you need:

- 3 bars laundry soap such as Zote, Fels-Naphtha, or Dr. Bronner's Pure-Castile Soap
- 64-oz box baking soda
- 76-oz box Borax
- 5 lb. container OxiClean
- 55-oz box washing soda

Cut the soap into pieces about the size of your thumbnail. The Zote soap is much moister than the Fels-Naphtha, and in the future, I'll most likely stick with the Fels because it chops into a nice powder. Another lovely-smelling and natural option would be Dr. Bronner's Pure-Castile soap.

Initially, I was using the dry canister of my blender for just the soap, but it was getting gummy instead of coarsely chopped. I resolved this by adding ½ cup of baking soda and a handful of cut-up soap and processing the two items together. Don't over-blend it, or it will still give you gummy chunks.

Then comes the ridiculously easy part. Dump all of your ingredients into a container big enough to mix it in—I used a large Rubbermaid tub and two big cooking spoons. Once it is well mixed, transfer it into the container in which you intend to store it.

**Instructions for use:**
I saved the scoop from the OxiClean container. Half of the scoop is 3 table-spoons, which is more than enough soap per load. With powdered laundry detergent, some people prefer to fill the washing machine and agitate the soap for a few minutes to dissolve it. I just chuck it in on top of the clothes, start the machine, and walk away, and it dissolves just fine. This is dependent on the hardness of your water, so you'll need to experiment for best results. I have used this recipe with both an older, top-loading machine and a newer, front-loading high efficiency machine and it worked splendidly in both.

That's it! What are you waiting for?

## How Decluttering Can Help You Be More Frugal

Let's talk about clutter.

I haven't seen my car keys for a week now. I misplaced them when I was working on this book. I was focusing so hard that my house got messy and I'm assuming they're hidden somewhere in the midst of the chaos. This got me thinking about how decluttering can help you save money. Beyond the obvious point of finding my car keys instead of replacing them, there are all sorts of benefits I've noticed while going through my house and decluttering as part of my spring-cleaning frenzy.

Here they are, in no particular order.

- **When you have less, it's easier to find things.** This saves time as well as money. Your keys, library books, and rented movie DVDs are all easy to locate, you don't spend hours turning the place upside down looking for the items, and you don't have to pay fines or replace them.

- **You can make good money selling the stuff you don't need.** Do you have too many kitchen tools that you never use? What about clothing that is a size you haven't been since you were nineteen? Do you have electronic gadgets that no one in the family uses anymore? List these items on Craigslist or Facebook Market. Or, you can have a yard sale to rake in the cash. Your clutter could be someone else's treasure.

- **Living in a clutter-free environment is less stressful.** And we all know that stress often pushes us to spend money on things we don't need, shouldn't eat, or didn't actually want in the first place.

- **You don't have to replace things that simply got misplaced.** Have you ever bought ingredients that you knew you already had, but you just couldn't find? Or bought new razors although you were positive you just grabbed another pack on your last trip to the store? If your items are well-organized and easy to find, say goodbye to the duplicate purchases and save your money for things you *really* need.

- **You don't have to spend as much money organizing your stuff when you have less stuff.** If you have tons of things, you probably also spend a significant amount of money containing those things. Shelving units, Rubbermaid tubs, drawer organizers, and cubbies all cost money and the more stuff you have, the more it will cost you to keep it organized.

- **You need more room when you have more stuff.** That means if you are renting or buying a new home, you may have to get a bigger (read: more expensive) place to live, just to stash your stuff. Plus, the more belongings you have, the more expensive it is to relocate it. Some people have outgrown their spaces so much that they must rent storage units for the stuff they aren't even using.

- **You save time when your home is clutter-free.** How much time have you spent "looking" for things recently? I have spent hours searching for my car keys—hours that could have been spent more productively. If you spend fifteen minutes per day looking for things, you've spent more than *ninety hours* over the course of a year. Ninety hours that could have been used in amazingly productive ways! How often do we look for shortcuts that cost more money because we don't have "time" to do the from-scratch, longer way? Ninety hours!

I'd write more, but now I'm feeling motivated to declutter.

## Fifteen Reusable Options for Stuff That Most People Throw Away

We live in a society driven by convenience. Fast food businesses thrive while home cooking flounders. Trips to the pharmacy can now be undertaken without getting out of your car, using the handy drive-through. Standard cleaning products are quickly being overtaken by disposable items you toss in the trash after one use.

We've been brainwashed by the marketing companies to believe that the simplest things are wildly inconvenient, and that in our time-crunched society we must pay for shortcuts. All this convenience has a high price tag. Not only are you spending money unnecessarily at the checkout counter for it, but the planet is getting buried under mountains of rubbish. The average American produces 1,600 pounds of garbage per year.

Did you ever stop to think about how many disposable things you buy? We do our shopping monthly instead of weekly, and this makes it a lot more noticeable on our bill when we load up with things that will be thrown out. I just checked the price, and a six-pack of good quality paper towels would add about $8 to my bill. If you're in a position in which every penny counts, that $8 could be buying you a necessity like food. Even if you have no concern about the landfills, you're here because you want to save money, right? Pennies each week add up to dollars each month, and hundreds of dollars over the course of a year.

**The fifteen things you'll never have to buy again.**
It probably goes without saying that if you're on a strict budget, you should not be buying silly things like cleaning wipes for the counters, paper plates, disposable dusters, and, for crying out loud, disposable toilet brushes. However, there are lots of other conveniences that can be just as easily replaced with reusable items.

If you aren't desperately trying to cut expenses, you might look at some of these and say "Yuck, not for me, thank-you-very-much!" But if times are tight, every penny counts.

**Coffee filters:** We love coffee in our family. There's a pot on for most of the day every day. Not only do we have a conventional drip coffee maker, but we also have a Keurig for a quick cup in the afternoon. Here's the awesome thing: you can get reusable filters for both for well under $10. We've replaced the throwaway paper filters for our coffee pot with a little mesh basket that also comes in a pointy version if your coffee maker uses the cone type of filter. If you have a Keurig, you can get reusable pods. This saves money by allowing you to use your own high-quality coffee at a fraction of the cost of K-cups. I keep these filled and in the fridge so that I can have a quick cup of afternoon coffee without spending 75 cents for it.

**Napkins:** This is a no-brainer. We have a lovely collection of cloth napkins, many of which have been purchased at yard sales or thrift stores. I don't get fabrics that require ironing (Yep, I made that mistake before!) and we simply toss them in the hamper just off the kitchen when they need to be washed. I think they look so much prettier on the table than the paper kind.

If it isn't yard sale season, you can start out with a dozen inexpensive ones from Amazon or your local discount store. Some people like to stick to white so that stains can easily be bleached out. I prefer a colorful variety. If you plan to use them for more than one meal, each family member could be assigned a color so that you know which napkin belongs to which person.

**Paper towels:** During the most broke point of my life, I decided that paper towels were completely unnecessary when they meant the difference between buying a roast that would feed my family for several days or not. I use—gasp—towels. I'm a big fan of the bar mop type of towels for cleaning. They're very absorbent and soak up big spills quickly and easily.

**Feminine hygiene products:** Avert your eyes, gentleman readers. Breaking news: tampons and disposable pads are actually not necessary for life as a woman. Women had monthly cycles well before Tampax formed a company to convince them that a disposable product was imperative.

There are lots of different options, including fabric pads, feminine cups, and natural sea sponges that just get rinsed out and reused. You can get washable, waterproof bags for storing the used pads if you are away from home that are designed to keep moisture and odor contained. These are all actually much healthier than commercial tampons and pads that contain all sorts of toxic "absorbent" materials.

**Razors:** Most of us shave some part of our bodies and go through tons of those expensive, plastic disposables. You can splurge on a good quality safety razor that will last for years and the only thing you'll need to replace (and dispose of) are the blades themselves. It will only take a couple of months' worth of disposable razors for this investment to pay for itself.

**Diapers:** With baby number 1 we lived in a tiny second story walk-up with no washer and dryer, so I used a combination of disposable and cloth diapers. With baby number 2, our circumstances had improved and we had our own washer and dryer, so I cheerfully embraced cloth diapers 100 percent of the time.

The cloth diapers today are so much better than the ones our grand-parents used. They have liners, snaps, different sizes, and all sorts of conveniences to make a mama's life easier. In fact, they look a lot like disposables. You can often pick these up secondhand since they can't be used for other purposes like the old-fashioned foldable diapers. While the initial purchase is an investment, if you're committed to using cloth, you will save hundreds of dollars throughout your child's diaper days.

**Cosmetic wipes:** Use washcloths. I don't have any snazzy how-tos or advice, except that we have black washcloths specifically for removing eye makeup so that you don't see any mascara stains.

**Baby wipes:** Soft baby washcloths can be dampened and stored in a ziplock bag when you're on the go. (Be sure to remember a bag for the dirty cloths, too.) Your baby wipe cloths can be soaked in the same bucket as the diapers and washed in the same load.

**Dryer sheets:** Replace dryer sheets but still have soft clothing with those nifty dryer balls, or clean, unused tennis balls. Even a crumpled piece of alu-minum foil can be tossed in to remove static cling, and that same piece of foil will be good for up to six months.

You can make your own dryer balls using 100 percent wool yarn. I like to scent them with a little bit of essential oil so that I get a lovely clean smell without the nasty dryer sheet chemicals. (My favorite scent is a mix of basil and lavender—trust me, it's fresh and delightful! )

**Lunch bags:** Everyone is enamored with the pretty lunch bags that almost look like purses, but you can take it a step further. Get rid of the plastic sand-wich and snack baggies and use fabric ones that can be tossed in the wash or rinsed out when you're doing dishes. You can even make your own in about fifteen minutes.

Of course, only you can judge whether or not these will make it home. If your kids toss them in the trash or lose them, the fabric version will be exponentially more expensive. In that case, just rewash the plastic bags that make it home.

**Food wrap:** Forget the Saran Wrap and look for other ways to keep leftovers in the refrigerator. I particularly like "Bees Wrap" which is made from fabric coated in beeswax. To make your own, all you need is a few supplies and pinking shears. The warmth of your hands makes the wrap cling.

**Shopping bags:** In some areas, stores now charge for shopping bags. At 10 cents a pop, this can add up over the course of a year to well over $50. (It could be far more depending on how much you buy.) Stash some reusable bags in your car so that you always have them available. You can buy them fairly inexpensively but making your own from old T-shirts or miscellaneous fabric can be a fun (and free) project to do with kids.

**Swiffer covers:** When we lived on a dusty, dirty farm with a cat and dog that came into the house, our floors needed to be dust-mopped every single day. I liked the convenience of a Swiffer, but not the expense of the disposable covers for it. With machine-washable covers, I could use a fresh one each time I dust-mopped. You can even make them from cotton socks. Finally, a way to make use of those lonely, single socks!

**Water bottles:** Do you know how many water bottles get thrown out each year? More than *22 billion!* That is almost an unfathomable amount. Purchasing water in individual bottles is awfully hard on the budget, too. If it isn't too toxic, you can filter your tap water and fill your own bottles. If you must purchase your water, go with the 5-gallon refillable jugs, and dispense it into your own BPA-free bottles. My kids are older, and we use glass bottles with a neoprene sleeve for protection.

**Batteries:** With flashlights, remotes, and other gadgets, we go through about a jillion batteries a year, although less than when my kids were little and had battery operated toys. We use almost exclusively rechargeable batteries. While they're more expensive on the front end, these have to be purchased far less frequently and can save you a bundle over time. Look for a charger that works for everything from AAA to 9V. Some even work on non-rechargeable batteries.

**When every penny counts, don't throw away money.**
If your budget is tight like mine, every single penny counts. Be sure to spend your money wisely by investing in reusable items, making the ones you can, and hitting the thrift stores to channel our frugal grannies.

**Do you have too much house and not enough money?**
All of the preceding ideas are great, but they cannot overcome a home that is too expensive itself. A major issue these days is too much house and not enough money to pay for it. In the 80s and 90s, everyone's goal seemed to be to build or buy a McMansion whether they had a large family or not. For some of us, our home became too big as our kids left and went off to make lives for themselves. Sure, it's great to have a guest room, but you probably don't need three of them.

A bigger house is more expensive in many ways:

- Higher property taxes
- More maintenance on house and lawn
- Higher utility bills
- Bigger mortgage payments

You should take a hard look at where you're living and decide whether you are spending more than you should on your home. Are you living in a fancy neighborhood with high HOA fees? Is your home too big? Is your yard too much work? It's not feasible for everyone to just pick up and move—we'll get to that in a moment. But if you discover you have a home that you simply can't afford, it may be time to consider downsizing. One way to do that is to move to a smaller house in the same town. Contrary to what they may tell you, no child ever died because he or she had to share a room with a sibling. You can live without a living room, family room, and rec room in the same house. A smaller home is easier to care for whether you're cleaning it or repairing it.

Another way to downsize is to relocate to a small town if you are currently a city dweller. Check to find if it it's worthwhile to commute to a job in the city from a smaller, less expensive location. This can give you the added opportunity of growing a garden and maybe raising a few hens to provide for more of your own needs.

Some things to consider before downsizing are:

- How far will you have to drive for work?
- Will you be able to find work in your new location?
- Are the kids at a point when changing schools will not be harmful?
- Is your spouse on board?
- What is the property tax situation in your desired area?
- Will you actually save money in the smaller home?
- Will you have to sell your current home at a loss, or do you have enough equity for a down-payment?
- How is the real estate market where your current home is located?
- If you rent, when is your lease over?
- How much will it cost to move?
- How soon will you recoup your moving costs with a lower mortgage?

The answer is different for every family. For me, moving to a two-bedroom cabin in the boondocks was the answer for me to get my feet on the ground, get a kid through college, and start a new career. But it may not be the same for you. This a huge decision, so make it carefully.

If you can't move right away, look at other options for making your living situation more affordable, like taking in boarders or a roommate. Can you set up a little apartment in the basement for a renter? Dramatic savings require dramatic changes.

## How to Move the Frugal Way

If you decide that relocation is in order, now's your chance to get rid of what you don't need and organize what you do need. Sorting through all your belongings and packing is the biggest job when undertaking a move. Over the years, you may have accumulated a lot of "stuff." Thrifty people tend to keep things that we may be able to use in the future. We dismantle no-longer-working items for the spare parts, we save buttons and rubber bands, and we have stockpiles of all sorts.

It's hard to discard those "things that might be useful someday," but the less stuff you move, the less it costs. Especially in a long-distance move, every-thing you take costs money. It takes up valuable space on the moving van and the additional weight of each item uses gas. For some things, it will be cheaper to replace them on the other end.

When sorting through the contents of your house, you need to ask yourself a few questions before you discard it:

### Would I be able to easily replace this in the future?

I get a lot of my things at yard sales and thrift stores, and this makes some of them tough to replace. For example, I have an antique coffee grinder, an adorable little device with a hand crank. I picked it up for $3, cleaned it, and now use it on a regular basis in my kitchen. It could be tough to replace because of the age and condition, so my beloved coffee grinder has always made the cut.

On the other hand, I have a toaster that I still use even though only one side actually works now. (Yes, I am so ~~cheap~~ thrifty that I turned the bread partway through the toasting time for a year.) I could easily find another one (that works!) for just a few dollars at a thrift store, though, so when I move, the toaster is history.

### How much would it cost to replace this in the future?

This is a similar concept to question #1. A collection of shampoos and soaps from the dollar store will take up a lot of space and can quickly and easily be replaced in the future. When I moved from Canada to the US, my oldest daughter, who was starting college, became the beneficiary of a host of cleaning supplies, health and beauty aids, and small appliances.

Other items that did not make the cut were inexpensive bulk-purchased beans and rice, canned goods, and eighteen-year-old bath towels that had been moved numerous times to sit in the back of numerous closets, waiting for the day they were needed.

Finally, most of our furniture was "vintage," which is a nice way of saying that it came from yard sales and the occasional curbside pile. It was more logical for us to refurnish from yard sales when we arrived at our new home, rather than moving our motley assortment of household paraphernalia.

### Is it worth the space in the moving van?

How you choose the importance of an item is a personal decision for everyone. Some things aren't particularly useful, but they are sentimental—gifts from departed loved ones and photo albums, for example. A great way to save space is to pack clothing and linens in "space bags." When you do that, you can stuff a lot more into a smaller space.

**How will you get to your new home?**

There are many options for moving your household.

- Hire movers (the most expensive option)
- Rent a moving van and drive it yourself
- Rent a moving "pod" (this will be cheaper on long-distance moves than paying for gas in a moving truck)
- Tow a trailer
- Ship your items—check Greyhound, Amtrak, airlines, and the USPS for rates (this is good if you only have a few boxes that won't fit in your vehicle)
- Take only what fits in your vehicle

Animals are another consideration. In some situations, like very long distances, you may want to fly unhappy travelers like cats. Our dog, on the other hand, is an enthusiastic traveler (not to mention a bit of added security), so she has hung out with us in the SUV, head cheerfully hanging out the window and breathing in the smells of two countries and seventeen states.

## The Move Itself

The end of the undertaking is near . . . your truck or trailer is loaded up with all of your worldly possessions. The kids are buckled in, and the dog has her head hanging out the window. There are some considerations for the road trip itself.

- Bring food with you. It's way cheaper and healthier than getting fast food throughout the entire trip.
- Bring a cooler with drinks instead of buying water bottles at $2 a pop each time you stop for gas.
- Go camping. If your family enjoys camping, stop at campgrounds instead of hotels for a much less expensive sleep during a long trip.
- Don't get lost—use a GPS or maps to stay on course.
- Make sure your vehicle maintenance has been taken care of before your departure.
- Don't let the fuel level drop below ¼ of a tank—in remote areas, gas stations can be few and far between.

Use common sense safety measures during the road trip:

- Keep the kids within view of an adult at all times.
- Keep a cell phone charged in case you need to call for help. (If you are like me and don't use cell phones, consider the purchase of an inexpensive TracFone for the trip.)
- Always have plenty of drinking water in the vehicle, especially in hot weather.
- Follow the rules of the road.
- Choose stopping points and parking spaces carefully and consider cracking the window of your room if you are staying in a motel, so that you can hear what is going on outside.
- Pay attention to your surroundings—ditch the headphones and remain alert during rest stops.
- Keep your truck or trailer locked at all times.
- Follow your gut—if you have a bad feeling about a situation, chances are, you're right.

# Part Five
# I Chose the Frugal Life

There are a lot of things about living frugally you can chalk up to habit. It's just the way you do things now. When frugality becomes second nature, things will be far easier.

## It's the Little Habits That Make You Truly Frugal

It's the little things, not the big ones, that make you a true Frugalite. When most people start moving toward a thriftier lifestyle, they tend to look at the big picture. They ask things like, "How can I save money on my car?" or "How can I pay less for that new laptop?" These are all fine things to do. Paying less is great, but shopping for a bargain is actually not the key to a frugal lifestyle.

If you're a full-fledged Frugalite, you know that living a life of thrift and frugality is all about the little habits. It's about your mindset. Saving money on enormous expenditures is great, but it is the small daily actions that add up and change your life. Truly frugal people absolutely *love* saving money. Embrace these habits and make them your own. You'll soon see an incredible difference in the way you look at pretty much everything.

**Frugalites use everything right to the last drop.**
If you go to someone's home and notice that their ketchup bottles are upside down in the refrigerator, their toothpaste tube on the bathroom counter is tightly rolled and held in place with a clothespin, and the contents of the liquid soap pump look mysteriously watery, you may be visiting a fellow Frugalite.

We don't like to waste stuff, so we use things right to the last drop, until there is absolutely no life left in it. We use rubber spatulas to get one more sandwich from the peanut butter jar. (I even have a special skinny rubber spatula that I purchased for the express purpose of scraping out containers in the kitchen.) We extend our dish soap with a little bit of water.

What others throw away, *we* see as a personal challenge. I don't know about you, but I get a little rush seeing how many more bangs I can get for my buck when using things that most folks would consider empty.

### Frugalites like to stay home.

I'm not saying that you need to be a hermit on a mountaintop, trekking into the village on foot once a year for salt, sugar, and a box of oranges to offset scurvy, but you don't have to go out every single day. If you have the day off, why not enjoy your home and your family instead of heading out to an activity that is going to cost money for admission, refreshments, and a snazzy item from the gift shop?

### Frugalites don't spoil their children.

This may not make you popular now, but later, your kids just might appreciate it. When my kids were in public school, I was astonished at the cost of various activities and events. There were $40 field trips, $5 "pizza days," and special $50 hoodies adorned with the school emblem. As a single mom with two kids in school, there was no way I was just forking out the money for this stuff. So, when the girls came home with forms and asked for money, I made a list of extra chores they could do around the house to earn the money for the activity. If they didn't feel it was worth a little extra work for them, I certainly wasn't going to hand them my hard-earned cash for it.

They learned the value of work, the relationship between work and getting stuff, and that sometimes, what they paid for just wasn't worth the effort of earning the money for it. As well, they came to appreciate special meals and activities more. A while back, I took them on a vacation and splurged a little. I was touched by how appreciative they were and delighted as I saw them take steps to keep expenses down, like packing a picnic in our little hotel kitchenette instead of planning to eat out all day.

When a child is constantly given everything, they grow up to be less satisfied, and they're a lot harder to make happy. Those are the kids who grow up to be the adults that trade their cars in every two years and keep remortgaging their homes for things like pools and pricey vacations. It is far more loving to raise your children in an atmosphere that encourages thrift, productivity, and personal accomplishment instead of a silver platter environment.

**Frugalites have productive hobbies.**

What do you like to do for fun? Does it use up resources or produce them? Productive hobbies should teach something, create something, repair something, or improve something. Most of my hobbies are relatively productive. Sure, I'll watch a movie on Netflix, but while I do, I'm crocheting a Christmas present, mending clothes, or making some small item for our home. I like to grow vegetables and flowers. Chickens make me happy.

**Frugalites don't shop as a form of entertainment.**

When you shop as "something to do" you are bound to spend money on something you don't need. I have daughters, and they really don't love my theory on this, but we shop when we need to get something. We don't just go hang out at the mall. When it was time to buy some school clothes, I allotted a certain amount of money and time, and when it was gone, it was gone. I do the same thing with Christmas shopping.

The mall is fraught with ways to drain your money—you get thirsty and buy a bottle of water or another drink. You weren't hungry but the smells from the food court are so tantalizing you can't resist. That display in front of the store has doohickeys that are *only* a dollar. Remember that these days, you don't have to physically be at the mall to be tempted. Websites like Amazon are loaded with ways to part you and your money.

**Frugalites save pennies throughout every single day.**

Cheapskatery is a way of life for us. It isn't all about saving money on the big things. It is eagerly grasping hold of the challenge of doing everything less expensively. It's automatically calculating the lowest unit price. It's making things instead of buying them. It's choosing to use your own creativity instead of the party supply store's when throwing a birthday party for your child. It's putting on a sweater instead of turning up the heat. These small daily actions add up to enormous savings and allow you, unlike the great majority of our society, to live within your means.

**Frugalites put aside emergency funds.**

When times are tight, being taken by surprise over a sudden necessity is sure to turn your budget upside down if you haven't prepared for it. This is why frugal people keep a rainy-day fund and a fully-stocked pantry. Then, if the refrigerator groans and breathes its last, if the car grinds to a halt 50 miles from home, or if a family member needs to go to the doctor, you don't have to decide whether to deal with the emergency or keep your electricity on.

### Frugalites cook from scratch.

One of the most certain ways to destroy your budget is to eat food prepared by other people. Think about it: whether you buy it from a restaurant or from a box on the grocery store shelf, someone spent time making that food. And you are paying for that! Those pouches of pre-cooked rice, those rotisserie chickens, that bag of take-out food, or that just-add-water and heat for 10 minutes meal from a box all include the cost of someone else's labor. If you don't know how to cook from scratch, there are simple foods you can start with like soup, steamed vegetables, baked potatoes, and chicken breast. Get an old-fashioned cookbook for simple instructions to make basic foods.

### Frugalites do things the low-tech way.

There are simple ways to save money that don't show you an immediate return, but the savings sure do add up. Things like hanging your laundry instead of using your dryer. Things like taking it easy in the hottest part of a summer afternoon instead of cranking up the air conditioner. Things like using solar lights as night lights. The list could go on and on, but by reducing your dependence on electricity and natural gas (or whatever your heat source is) you can save hundreds of dollars per year.

### Frugalites repair things.

We live in a society of planned obsolescence. Most things aren't made to last a lifetime anymore, and our society is happy to just toss their doodads in a landfill and go get new ones. Frugalites fix things. We mend our clothes, we repair our appliances, we fix broken furniture, and some of us even do unheard of things like darning our socks. We don't immediately think about replacement. Our first step is always repair.

### Real frugality is all in your head.

Hardcore frugality is not just making a choice to buy the generic brand of laundry soap instead of a jug of Tide with scent beads. Hardcore frugality is buying the ingredients to make five times the amount of laundry soap for half the price of that name-brand detergent, all the while *loving* the fact that Procter & Gamble are not getting your money.

Being a black belt in frugality takes creativity and an optimistic outlook. It should never be some grim, sad thing that you have to do. It should be something that you choose to do. By finding joy in your non-consumerism, you will be far more successful at it. It becomes a game that you win if you can do something for free that others spend money on.

When you feel like you require less, in turn you are happy with less. This means that you have to spend less time working at things you may not truly enjoy to pay for the things that you never actually needed in the first place. This means that the money you have goes a lot further and that your life feels a lot more satisfying.

When you finally cross that line between resenting the fact that you have to strictly budget to embracing the fact that by being as thrifty as possible, you have achieved freedom you never dreamed of before, you've made the conversion. You aren't just acting with thrift until things get better. You, my friend, are one of those truly joyous Frugalites that others look to for inspiration.

## *More* Things You Can Reuse That Most Folks Throw Away

It's no secret that we live in a throwaway society. Americans create about 250 *tons* of garbage every single year. And we throw out a *lot* of stuff that could be reused. Maybe this is Frugalite 101, but I wanted to write about all the things we throw out that could safely be used again, often many times.

**Plastic sandwich bags:** If you use those little plastic sandwich bags, do you consider them disposable? Unless they've held raw meat, something rotten, or something toxic, they can easily be washed and reused. I turn them wrong side-out and rinse them in the sink before I do dishes. Then, I scrub them with a sponge. Rinse them in your rinse water.

I have a dryer for these babies that I made out of Tinkertoys. No, I'm not kidding. I have Tinkertoys on my counter and no little kids. You can make a grownup version with some thin doweling placed in a tall glass.

**Tinfoil:** Why would you throw out perfectly good tinfoil just because you've used it once? I straighten it out flat, lay it on the counter, and wipe it with my dishcloth. Once it's dry, I fold it up and stick it in the foil drawer.

**Plastic shopping bags:** Just about everyone I know has a huge stash of plastic bags under their kitchen sink, and often, out of frustration, they scoop up all umpteen million of them and toss them in the trash. (Or maybe that's just me.) These bags can be reused in multiple ways:

- Line your bathroom garbage can.
- Toss your scooped poop from the cat litter in them.
- Store some in your car so you don't keep bringing more of them home.
- Donate them to your local thrift store—they're always in need of bags.
- My mother-in-law and the ladies at her church cut them into long strips and crochet mats out of them. The multipurpose mats are sturdy and water resistant. The ones she made were being handed out to homeless people to keep another layer between them and the cold ground.
- Use them for packing material if you are mailing something or moving.

**Egg cartons:** There are all sorts of ways you can keep from throwing out egg cartons. I use them to start seedlings in the spring. They're nice for popping into a drawer to hold jewelry, tiny craft supplies, beads, or sewing notions. Also, anyone you know who has chickens (including vendors at the farmers' market) will appreciate getting some egg cartons for free.

**Glass jars:** I'm thinking about jars beyond mason jars you'd use for canning. What about jars that once held sauces, jams, or olives?

- Clean them well and use them for canisters and storage containers in your kitchen. For a uniform look, you can spray paint the lids the same color. You can even spray paint them with chalkboard paint for easy labeling.
- Use them as vases for flowers.
- Use them as drinking glasses.
- Plop a tealight candle in them for your table outdoors. This way the wind won't blow them out.

**Old clothes**: Donate anything that is in good shape, because someone else might really be able to use those items. But those old clothes that are too rough to donate? Wait a second before tossing them out! The obvious choice is to cut them up into rags for cleaning. But . . . you can also deconstruct them:

- Cut off the buttons for your button jar
- Take it apart at the seams to get pieces of fabric you can reuse
- Cut some squares from the good part of the fabric for quilting or other small projects
- Trim strips for rag rugs
- Remove any decorative patches or appliques for future use
- Unravel old sweaters for some useful yarn
- If you have old blankets or towels, donate them to your local animal shelter

**Plastic cutlery:** If you get takeout from time to time, you likely get plastic cutlery along with it. We generally put it aside and use our regular flatware. If you *do* use plastic cutlery, you don't have to discard the items after one use. However, only use them a few times, as the plastic degrades with repeated washing.

- Wash them and put them aside for school lunches. (That way if the fork or spoon doesn't make it home, it's no big loss.)
- Use them for plant markers in the garden—write on them with a Sharpie so you can remember what you planted.
- Use them when you're stirring up things like hair dye or craft paint.
- Search online—there are all sorts of creative crafts that can be done with plastic cutlery.

**Dryer sheets:** I know that not everyone uses dryer sheets for a multitude of reasons. But if *you do* use them, they don't have to be thrown away after one use.

- You can use them for one or two more loads of laundry.
- Put them inside shoes when you take them off to keep them smelling nice and fresh.
- Place them inside your dresser drawers for a hint of scent.
- If you have pets, use them for dusting or running along the baseboards. They pick up the fur like magic.

**Plastic food containers:** If you don't heat these up, they can easily be reused for a multitude of purposes. If you tend to avoid plastic, you can use them for non-food storage as well.

- Use them like Tupperware for leftovers. *Do not reheat your food in these containers.* They aren't made to withstand heat and can leach chemicals into your food. *Hint*: Little is more annoying than grabbing what you think is the sour cream and finding out that it's actually last night's lasagna. Avoid this frustration by mixing up the lids. Put a yogurt lid on the butter tub and a butter lid on the sour cream tub.
- Use them to start seedlings.
- Flip the lids upside down to use as impromptu coasters.
- Use them in the craft room or workshop to hold little bits and bobs. Label them with a Sharpie.

And there you have it. All sorts of ideas to get your wheels turning!

## Essential Skills Every Frugalite Should Have

As some of you know, the other thing I write about is emergency preparedness. One thing I have discovered that really crosses between the two fields of prepping and frugality is *skills*. You can have all the supplies in the world but if you don't have the skills and knowledge to use them properly, they won't help you much in an emergency. You can restrict your spending all you want, but if you don't have the skills to create or fix things, there is a limit to how much you can save. This brings me to a list of essential skills that every Frugalite should cultivate.

**Cooking from scratch:** If you're not cooking from scratch using basic ingredients, then you are paying someone else to do it for you. You don't have to have a personal chef to be contributing to the labor of another person. If your freezer is loaded with meals prepared by someone else, you paid for them to make that meal. If your cake came from the bakery, you paid someone to bake it, assemble it, and decorate it. If your apple slices are already cut up or your lettuce is washed and put in a bag, you've paid for the labor of someone else.

Now, I'm not saying that you can never ever use any convenience foods, but when you do, know that you are paying more for that convenience. Learning to cook from scratch is one of the most money-saving practical skills ever for a budding Frugalite. If you are new to scratch cooking, look *waaay* back and grab yourself a Fannie Farmer cookbook or something else from that era. These books were written in the early 1900s before every recipe contained a conveniently boxed ingredient and deboned chicken.

**Acquiring food outside the grocery store:** There are all sorts of ways to acquire food that don't involve the grocery store and doing so seems to be a lost art. Think back to the days of your ancestors. How did they keep the family fed? It certainly had nothing to do with the words "Kroger" and "Safeway."

A few alternative ways to acquire food are:

- Gardening
- Raising fruit trees
- Raising livestock
- Hunting
- Fishing
- Trapping
- Foraging

You may not wish to do all of these things but adding at least a couple of them to your repertoire can help you cut your budget by acquiring food on your own.

**Sewing:** You don't have to go full-on *Little House on the Prairie* and dress in handmade garments made from flour sacks to make use of sewing skills. You can still use that skill for things like:

- Mending torn or damaged clothing
- Hemming things that are too long
- Letting out the hem on things that are too short
- Making alterations to garments that don't fit properly
- Making specialty outfits like Halloween costumes or dress-up clothes
- "Upcycling" worn clothing into things like purses, scarves, quilts, or doll clothes
- Making home décor items like curtains or placemats
- Making much-envied gifts that are exactly what the recipient wanted but couldn't find in the store

Also, in the category of sewing, I'd put things like crocheting, knitting, and embroidering. Making or updating clothing, home décor items, and accessories yourself can save you a lot of money.

**DIY:** DIY is not only satisfying, but it can be a lot of fun, too. You can apply DIY skills to home décor, home repair, fashion, and much, much more.

Here are some of the skills a good DIYer might have:

- Painting
- Faux finishing
- Gluing (I know, not much of a skill but you'd be surprised how many people never think of gluing something in place!)
- Carving
- Woodwork
- Decorating
- Soldering
- Beading
- Crafting

This also ties in with some of the skills above, like sewing and building. The great thing about DIY projects is that if you're smart, you can use supplies you already have on hand to create something brand new. Of course, if you go buy all new supplies, your DIY project won't be very thrifty. There are loads of wonderful websites about upcycling that can help you develop a fun and inexpensive new hobby.

**Building:** Can you build stuff? I'm not talking about entire houses (although that would be great too)! I mean smaller things that you'd have to pay a lot of money to buy already made. Dog houses, chicken coops, bookcases, kitchen islands, dining tables, decks . . . there are many things we need these days that cost a fortune when someone else builds them for you.

This is the exact same thing as having someone else prepare your food. You are paying for their labor. Instead, learn to make these things yourself. Start off simply and as your skills increase, so can the complexity of your projects.

**Home repair:** Have you ever had the furnace repair guy come over and literally just flip a switch to get your heater humming right along again? And then paid them a hundred dollars for doing it? I have. About 15 years ago, my furnace apparently sighed its last breath. My budget was so tight it squeaked and when the repair man came, he was there for less than 10 minutes—and most of that time was him writing up the bill. I was heartbroken because it literally meant no groceries that week. (Fortunately, we had some stuff put back, but still.)

That was when I became determined to learn how to troubleshoot the systems in my home. I have since repaired a leaking roof, taken apart a kitchen drain, and fixed a thermostat. Any time something has broken since that fateful day, I've at least spent some time attempting to repair it myself before calling in reinforcements. This is not a natural talent for me, but with help from the Internet (God bless YouTube) I have been able to do repairs that would have cost me hundreds of dollars if I had to have a professional do it. Obviously, take all the necessary precautions like donning the proper protective gear, using the correct tools, and turning off the associated electrical breakers before embarking on a home repair spree.

**Car repair/maintenance:** Do you know how to change a tire? Do you know how to jumpstart a dead car battery? Can you change your oil? When times are tight, being able to perform basic maintenance tasks on your car can save you a bundle. It's messy and some of it is hard work, but it's very satisfying.

There are some automotive repair tasks you can do, too, like the replacement of non-computerized parts. But with the advent of all things electronic, some tasks can't be done at home without the ability to perform flash updates to get the devices working properly. (This is how the automotive industry has made the home mechanic obsolete.)

## The Frugalite's Survival Kit
I write about all sorts of survival kits on my website, but one I haven't written about is the one I have for all my thrifty activities. Without further ado, here are the things that every frugal soul should keep close at hand.

**Duct tape:** It sounds like a cliché, but there are so many things that duct tape can quickly repair. I have duct-taped the back of a sofa after it got ripped during a move, the leg of a table, tarps, backpacks, sneakers, and much, much more. Was it sexy and beautiful? No, probably not. But the value of your ability to eke out just a little bit more wear from an item cannot be overlooked.

**WD-40:** It doesn't have to be name brand. Any kind of lubricant can be worth its weight in gold. From silencing squeaks to making hinges and moving parts work again, lubricating fluid is a valuable repair asset.

**Black dye:** At least once a year, I run all of our black clothing through the washing machine with a package of black fabric dye. It makes faded clothes look brand-spankin' new. (Be sure to run a load of darks as your next load after this so that you don't stain light colored clothing.)

**Hot glue gun:** Not only can you use these for all sorts of DIY crafts, but you can also use it for a multitude of repairs. I have used my hot glue gun to "weld" plastic bread tags onto plastic clothing hampers that have split. I've also used it to repair shoes, books, and toys. A dollop on each side of a plastic hanger can give clothing a little something to cling to. I've even seen YouTube videos of people repairing electrical cords with hot glue, although I have not done this myself.

**Zip ties:** Plastic zip ties have a multitude of uses. I use them in my garden every year to hold my tomato tipis together and also to secure wobbly plants to the piece of bamboo I stuck in the ground to stabilize them. (Be sure not to tighten it too much—they need room to grow.)

You can use zip ties to make all sorts of redneck contraptions, like attaching a teeny flashlight to the side of your glasses or holding a trouble light overhead on the beams of your basement. You can also use them to tame the mass of cords at the back of your entertainment center. In a pinch, I have even been known to put my hair in a ponytail using zip ties. (This was back in the days when I worked in an automotive shop.)

**Staple gun:** What *can't* you do with a staple gun? I've used one to reupholster furniture, to cover a piece of plywood with fabric, to attach posters to backing before putting them in a frame, and to attach "skirts" over some lower kitchen cabinets with long-lost doors.

**Vinegar:** You can clean with it, cook with it, pickle with it, and kill weeds with it. It's as multipurpose as a kitchen item can get.

There are probably lots more of these thrifty tools, but I would personally feel lost without the ones above. I certainly didn't just get them and put them away—I use them all the time. Use this list as inspiration to put together your own frugal survival kit.

## The Frugalite's Guide to Productive Hobbies

There's no denying that for many of us, times are tight. Many homes have a basket by the door full of unopened bills. Bank accounts are in overdraft. Every week the charges at the grocery store are a little bit higher than the week before, and for less food. Kids want new clothes and that latest video game, the car needs to be fixed, and people's jobs are draining the very life from them.

It is vital to take time out of the day to relax. It rejuvenates you, improves your health, and calms your mind so that you can think more clearly. Relaxation, creative activities, and family time can actually be frugal endeavors, not distractions that take away from your efforts to make ends meet.

When you have a million and one things to do, though, sometimes it's difficult to force yourself to stop. This is because stress releases two hormones in your body: adrenaline and cortisol. Excesses of these hormones can cause blood pressure spikes, food cravings that lead to weight gain, and heart disease, to name just a few of the pitfalls. So, baby, you've got to unwind. You need a hobby.

**But not these hobbies.**

Beware, some hobbies end up costing you money with nothing to show for it. Lots of people spend their time doing things like playing golf or tennis, going to concerts or night clubs, playing pool in a bar, drinking alcohol with friends, or shopping. All of these things have their place, of course, but as a regular part of your daily routine, they can certainly add up in price. If you're already stressed about your finances, these hobbies will give you a brief respite, but in the end, just cause you more stress because of all of the money you've spent.

Other hobbies kill off a few brain cells as you sit there, passively entertained in an altered state in front of the television or a video game. These things may not really cost you a lot of money, but in the long run will do little to alleviate stress. Passivity actually opens up the door to your brain and allows you to be programmed—mass media uses this as a tool, by promoting ideas like the politically correct flavor of the month.

> . . . Advertisers have known about this for a long time and they
> know how to take advantage of this passive, suggestible brain state of

the TV viewer. There is no need for an advertiser to use subliminal messages. The brain is already in a receptive state, ready to absorb suggestions, within just a few seconds of the television being turned on. All advertisers have to do is flash a brand across the screen, and then attempt to make the viewer associate the product with something positive.[1]

It's important to choose your spare time activities in a manner that enhances your brain function, instead of reducing it. In a world where, for many, entertainment means playing on your iPhone or sharing photos on Facebook, opting for industry for your downtime can be an unusual choice. But, stepping outside the path of the herd and choosing productive hobbies is a great way to relax. What's more, if your brain is engaged in an activity while you view a television program or movie, then you are not as susceptible to messages, either subliminal or blatant. This means that you don't actually have to keep the TV turned off at night—you just need to refrain from zoning out in front of it.

Now, I can't say that I never indulge in a little bit of binge-watching. I do, on a regular basis. The difference is, I don't just sit there. Actually, I'm pretty much incapable of simply sitting there watching something. I take the time that we spend watching a show to accomplish those mindless things like mending, organizing my sewing basket, crocheting, repairing broken items, or completing a frenzy of food prep.

**A brief lesson from young Ben Franklin.**
In 1726, twenty-year-old Benjamin Franklin sought to cultivate his character. He listed off the thirteen virtues that he believed were important to living a good life, one of which was industry. Franklin wrote of this characteristic, "Industry: Lose no time; be always employed in something useful." He believed that the pursuit of productivity would build character and help the practitioner to lead a more successful and moral life. In his autobiography, Franklin wrote "I hope, therefore, that some of my descendants may follow the example and reap the benefit." Think back to the days before television. People worked hard all day long, producing food, cutting wood, cooking, hunting, building . . . it was a full-time job to survive and thrive. In the

---

1    "Your Brain Waves Change When You Watch TV," I Am Awake, Oct. 11, 2013, http://www.iamawake.co/your-brain-waves-change-when-you-watch-tv/

evenings, by candlelight, they could stop and put their feet up for a while. Books were not widely available like they are now, so families passed the time by performing stitchery, carving, making furniture, mending things, and creating items that made their lives more pleasant and beautiful. Sometimes a family member would read aloud, play an instrument, or sing. Time was of value and not to be wasted, and there was rarely money to spare on an "evening out."

**Opt for activities that enhance your frugality.**
Nearly 300 years later, we can apply Franklin's philosophy of industriousness and productivity to our lives today. When choosing leisure activities, consider opting for a productive hobby.

It should either . . .

- Teach something
- Create something
- Repair something
- Improve something

That leaves the door wide open to a broad range of choices. If you tend to be an overachiever, then you can relax without the guilt of worrying about all the things that you "should" be doing instead of chilling out. As a longtime student of cheapskatery, I've found that most people who are effectively frugal have hobbies which are productive, and don't enjoy wasting time, even leisure time. Often your hobby can even turn into an additional source of income. Many people have been extremely successful starting their own Etsy empires or participating in the craft show circuit.

**Some productive hobbies to choose from.**
Some of these hobbies can be an enjoyable way to pass the time or add to your economic bottom line, and they can provide beautiful, lower-cost options for gift-giving, which is a frugal bonus. Not only should you, yourself, be indulging in these pastimes, but you should be passing these skills on to your children. When you do, you are creating not only useful and lovely items, but irreplaceable family memories. Our living room is full of attractive baskets which all hide the supplies for various crafts and hobbies. Of an evening, you can most often find us creating while a movie or music plays in the background.

- Reading
- Sewing clothing, curtains, and soft furnishings
- Knitting, crocheting, and weaving
- Carving
- Repairing broken items
- Mending
- Making soap and other personal care items
- Building furniture
- Making pottery
- Cooking and baking
- Writing
- Drawing and creating art
- Playing an instrument
- Singing
- Making cards
- Making jewelry
- Fletching
- Gunsmithing
- Making ammo
- Welding and soldering
- Learning a language
- Caring for animals
- Playing a word, math, or strategy game
- Marksmanship (archery and firearms)
- Exercise
- Gardening
- Preserving food
- Practicing outdoor skills like hiking, camping, and foraging
- Hunting and fishing
- Automotive repair

This list is certainly not comprehensive. Think about things you could do in your spare time that are both enjoyable and productive.

## The Life-Changing Economy of Staying Home

Being thrifty demands some sacrifices. Being careful with your money means that you can't necessarily keep up with the Joneses. Trust me, though, the time will come when the Joneses would trade their big screen TVs, their brand-new SUVs and their fancy gym memberships in order to keep up with you.

One of the easiest ways to save money is also one of the simplest. For some people, it's one of the most difficult. Stay home. That's it—nothing fancy at all. Just stay home more. Now, before the flurry of emails begins, I'm not suggesting that you become a mad hermit up on a mountain, only trekking to the village on foot once a year to buy salt and sugar. In fact, when I first wrote this, I was on vacation with my daughters. (The first one in five years!)

Actually, being on vacation is what inspired me to write this. I noticed some of the little things we spend money on when we're out and about. Because I work from home, I am not "tempted" by all the things there are to spend money on very frequently. While I don't think that we should stop living and enjoying life, during your everyday, non-vacation life, there are a lot of financial benefits to finding most of your entertainment, companionship, and solace from the comfort of your home.

## Transportation

The first big savings of staying home more frequently is the cost of your transportation. When fuel prices skyrocket, you probably notice the pain each time you go to the pumps.

### Group your errands.

Obviously, you have to go to work and run errands. By grouping these things into fewer outings, however, you will save money on fuel. Stop by the grocery store on the way home from work instead of making a special trip on the weekend. If you go to a gym, go on the way to work and use the showers there. If your kids are involved in activities, consider doing some errands while they are engaged instead of dropping them off, going home, and going out again to pick them up.

### Walk.

Are you within walking distance of any of the things you have to do? If so, do it. Walk to the post office on your lunch break. Walk to work and school if you're near enough. Not only will your wallet thank you, so will your health.

## Food and Beverages

We used to live in a pretty rural area. We did our grocery shopping once a month because it was a drive of an hour and a half. While we always took some drinks and snacks, nearly every single time we ended up buying something during our time away. Maybe it was a treat like ice cream on a steamy summer or hot chocolate in the chilly winter or even lunch at a restaurant. Since it was only once a month, I planned this into the budget. However, when you're out every day, these treats really begin to add up.

**Bring your lunch, your drinks, and your coffee.**
When I worked outside the home, I always brought my lunch and refilled my water bottle at the cooler. Many of my coworkers went out for fast food every day at lunch. They came in with a drive-through coffee cup in their hands, and went to the vending machine for a coke and a bag of chips. When you hit a drive-through every time you go out the door, the price of leaving home goes up.

**When you grocery shop, make a plan.**
When you go out for the explicit purpose of buying food and beverages, it's best to make a list. Bring a drink with you, so you aren't tempted to grab an overpriced bottle of water. Eat before you go so that everything in the store doesn't look so delicious that it makes its expensive, full-price way into your cart.

## Entertainment
It seems like a lot of people can't have fun at home anymore. Maybe I have a warped perspective of fun, but I have always enjoyed gardening, doing arts and crafts with the kids, making popcorn and watching a movie together, or just reading a book.

Our society has become so overstimulated that people constantly require more and greater stimulation in order to not feel "bored." Take for example the folks who are glued to their iPhones while spending time at a place that should be entertaining in and of itself. We once saw an entire family at a restaurant, each with their own device out, eating food and ignoring one another. Because we don't go out that often, I guess it's more of a treat, so we are fully engaged in it.

**By learning to entertain ourselves simply we can get a lot more happiness out of a lot less money.**
By developing some productive hobbies, we can be creative while meeting needs. By being active in our pursuits instead of passively entertained, we can be healthier in mind and body.

**And while we're on the topic of entertainment, shopping should *not* be "entertainment."** When you shop as "something to do" you are bound to spend money on something you don't need.

## It's Not You, It's Them

Don't feel bad if you've read the suggestions above and recognized yourself People go to college for four to six years just to learn how to part you and your money. Advertising is a multi-billion-dollar industry. Western society is *based* on commercialism.

Back in 2015, research showed that consumers were exposed to between 4,000 and 15,000 advertisements per day.[2] And it's growing exponentially, because before that, a 2007 article in the New York Times said that the average city dweller was subjected to more than 5,000 ads every single day.[3] It's a barrage that hits you not only when leaving your house, but when turning on the radio, surfing the Internet, and watching television.

> Add this to the endangered list: blank spaces. Advertisers seem determined to fill every last one of them. Supermarket eggs have been stamped with the names of CBS television shows. Subway turnstiles bear messages from Geico auto insurance. Chinese food cartons promote Continental Airways. US Airways is selling ads on motion sickness bags. And the trays used in airport security lines have been hawking Rolodexes. Marketers used to try their hardest to reach people at home, when they were watching TV or reading newspapers or magazines. But consumers' viewing and reading habits are so scattershot now that many advertisers say the best way to reach time-pressed consumers is to try to catch their eye at literally every turn. "We never know where the consumer is going to be at any point in time, so we have to find a way to be everywhere," said Linda Kaplan Thaler, chief executive at the Kaplan Thaler Group, a New York ad agency. "Ubiquity is the new exclusivity."

---

2   Ron Marshall, "How Many Ads Do You See in One Day?" Red Crow Marketing, Sept. 10, 2015, https://www.redcrowmarketing.com/2015/09/10/many-ads-see-one-day/

3   Louise Story, "Anywhere the Eye Can See, It's Likely to See an Ad," New York Times, Jan. 15, 2007, https://www.nytimes.com/2007/01/15/business/media/15everywhere.html

Recognizing that you are the target of commercialism run amok is the first step in resisting the marketing schemes. Your awareness that you are being manipulated makes you less likely to think, *Wow, that sounds great! I have to have it!* Be sure that you are the one who decides where your money should be spent. Identify your priorities and goals and avoid the marketing machine as much as possible. By centering your life around your home, you can stay focused on your goals. You can begin to see your home as a retreat from the stressors of the world instead of a grim place you're trapped.

## How to Keep Your Frugal Mojo

I'm willing to bet that it's not just me. Even though frugality has changed my life for the better and allowed me to afford things I never should be able to on my income, sometimes I chafe at the restrictions. Don't get me wrong. Most of the time, frugality is fun. Cheapskatery is a challenge that I relish. Doing something for free or cheap that other people spend money on gives me a little rush and I feel like I've "won." But every once in a while, I wish I could spend freely without worrying about tomorrow.

Sometimes, I want to go crazy at the grocery store and buy stuff because I want it, not because it's on sale. Occasionally, I would like to splurge without the guilt. When I feel like that, my motivation to do the activities that keep things cheap is about zero. Do you ever lose your frugal mojo? These tips will help you stay motivated.

### Give yourself a break.

Sometimes we all need it. Look in your budget and see if there is room for a little splurge. I find that for me, the best splurges are activities and not things most of the time. If I go buy something, often it only makes me happy for an hour or two. (Like a little kid with too many Christmas presents.)

Obviously, there are some things that prove this wrong—yarn, for example, gives me a long period of enjoyment because not only do I get to spend time making something, I get to enjoy the something I made, too. But for the most part, if I'm going to spend some money, I grab my daughter and we head out on a road trip to have a little adventure. We might grab a meal out while we're gone, and we'll do something, like touring a local cavern or visiting a historic place. Then, you are out and enjoying yourself on a carefree day while making memories with the people you love.

I always still handle money carefully and don't allow this to give me permission to go hog wild. I withdraw cash from the ATM in the amount that I plan to spend and use my debit card *only* in the case of an emergency.

**Think about your goal.**
Whatever your goal is, whether it's early retirement, one parent staying home with the kids, being debt-free, putting your kid through college, leaving your job to go back to school, or moving to a dream location, keep that goal front and center. (I share the specifics of my own goal and exactly how I plan to get there on page 38.) Find pictures that represent your goal and put them everywhere. Nothing keeps your motivation higher than a glimpse at the reason you're living this life.

**Think about what happens if you quit.**
Sometimes a little negative reinforcement is in order, too. What if you stop your frugal momentum? Will you be in the same place doing the same thing in five years instead of reaching your dream? Will the interest on your debt have stacked up to the point that paying it off will be a lot more daunting? Will you lose important things, like your home or car? Will your child have to go into debt for his or her education? Knowing what you *don't* want is every bit as important as knowing what you *do* want.

**Spend time with like-minded people.**
Okay, let's face it. There's nothing that makes you feel worse than going places with a spendthrift who is worse than a frat boy with a keg trying to get all the girls to have "just one more drink." Teenagers and college kids are not the only ones who get peer pressured. With adults, it's just as bad, especially when you consider that those adults trying to get you to "live a little" may just want some justification for their own bad spending habits.

And it isn't only friends who can make you feel badly. I remember when I was a young mom going out with some relatives. They didn't really understand how desperate my financial situation was, and they'd constantly point out "great deals" for my little one and look at me disapprovingly when I didn't snap them up. I felt *horrible* after a day out with them because, even though it was unintentional, their constant urging to spend when I had nothing available left me feeling guilty and embarrassed.

The joy of likeminded friends is that they don't want to go out and frivolously spend money any more than you do. They'll be your partner in crime going to yard sales and thrift stores. They will cheer on your cheap solutions instead of staring at you with their mouths agape in horror.

### Indulge in frugality "porn."

No, get your mind out of the gutter. By "porn" I mean immerse yourself in frugality. Find websites to check out. Reread this book. Go to Pinterest and search up budget-friendly DIYs. Read Amy Dacyczyn's *Tightwad Gazette* yet again. The last thing you want to do is watch regular TV with all the commercials for things you don't need or flip through a magazine with all manner of designer things that cost more than you make in a month.

I like to keep a list of web destinations that will make me feel good about my frugal lifestyle. There are all sorts of sites out there dedicated to upcycling and frugal living that will make you feel inspired just looking at them.

### Think about how much better off you are now that you're in thrift mode.

This one is kind of mean, but also incredibly satisfying. If ever you're feeling like the last kid picked for the dodgeball game, sit there and add up what other people are spending on things you get cheaply or for free.

Indulge for a moment in a feeling of superiority as you calculate their probable monthly budget and compare it to what you figure they make for a living. Then think about how much debt they must be in to live their current lifestyle. If you resist the urge to rub it in their spendy little faces, nobody is hurt by this exercise and you'll feel smug and happy. (Hey, I warned you it was kind of mean, but be honest, wasn't it fun?)

### Remember how great thrift is for the environment.

Instead of focusing on being cheap, think about the environment. The awesome side effect of hardcore frugality is that it is much better for Mother Earth. We aren't out there buying stuff in plastic packaging to be discarded each week. Most of us put far less garbage out to the curb than our spendier friends. We buy things from thrift stores and yard sales that would otherwise be on the way to a landfill. We are like Neighborhood Greenpeace with our thrifty ways, right?

**Give to others.**

While things may be tight in your life right now, it's a pretty sure bet that there are other people who are in worse shape. Realizing this will make you feel fortunate instead of morose about your own situation.

Do you have some pantry goods that you could spare to help somebody less fortunate? Is there a good deed you could do, like mowing the elderly neighbor's lawn for her? Many people think that frugality rules out generosity, but I think it is just the opposite. It makes you really think about how hard it is to get by in the world these days and that makes you a much more compassionate person.

Even when I was incredibly broke, each week when we went to the grocery store, I would get my girls to pick out a package of pasta and a can of sauce to put in the food bank box near the exit of the store. We figured that would provide a warm meal to somebody that might not have one, and for the $2 it cost at the time, it was one small thing we could do for others. This helped my daughters too, because if you are able to help others, you can't possibly be that badly off, right?

Try these things when you're feeling unmotivated and you'll have your thrifty mojo back in no time.

## How Saving Money Is Sometimes Better Than Making Money

We live in a society in which we pay for convenience. The very best way to save money is to spend time. It's one or the other, and depending on your situation, one may be in your power while the other is not.

Take a pizza, for example. Someone, somewhere, has to do the work to create that pizza. It might be more than one person. But you pay for every set of hands involved in getting that meal in front of you. In a restaurant, you might be paying for the cook and for the server. If you tend to get convenience meals at the grocery store, you are paying for someone else to have made the dough and assembled the pizza that you will in turn place in the oven at home. But if you make that pizza yourself, you have taken the time to mix the ingredients, knead the dough, let it rise, punch it down, let it rise more, and finally roll it out onto your pizza stone or pan. Then you are spending your time making the sauce, spreading it on, and topping the pizza with your favorite meats, veggies, and cheeses. All in all, you'll probably spend about an hour of hands-on time making that pizza. And time is money.

So, let's take this down to dollars and cents. You might spend $30 to have that pizza at a restaurant or $15 to buy the pre-assembled pizza at the store. The ingredients are going to cost anywhere from $3 to $5. This means that your hourly wage for making that pizza at home is approximately, at minimum $10 an hour, and at maximum $25 an hour. Best of all, it's tax free and you know exactly what is in the pizza you make at home.

**Now, let's look at a bigger example.**

Let's take the average ten-hour workday (including commute, lunch breaks, etc.) Now spend that day productively at home. Here are some things you might do that other people pay for:

- Growing food: $20
- Preparing food from scratch: $30
- Yard work: $40
- Cleaning the house: $50
- Mending clothes and doing laundry: $20
- Childcare—all day, simultaneous with other tasks: $75 for two kids
- Bathing and grooming the dog: $65
- Walking the dog at lunchtime: $10
- Making your own cleaning products and health and beauty aids: $20

If you add all of those things up, you are talking about a *lot* of money. I based my totals on the prices of those services and goods in my area, and on an average day, I could "earn" $330. Tax free. On an annual basis of a five-day work week, that is the equivalent of just over *$85,000 per year*. Again, let me reiterate *tax free*, which can save you another 15 to 30 percent.

Okay, I know that is not absolutely practical math and that people who work outside the home also do many of these things along with their workplace responsibilities. The point is, we all pay for conveniences unless we make a concentrated effort not to do so. We have all purchased laundry detergent at the store for twenty times what it costs to make a cheap and healthy version at home. We have all grabbed a frozen pizza to make our lives easier on a busy day. When we work outside the home (or when we have a challenging schedule in our home-based business), most of us have to pay someone to care for our children if we aren't lucky enough to have family around to help out. All of this stuff adds up, and some of it can't be helped.

**Spend time instead of money.**
It's vital, though, to look at the savings you are able to make, as money. Spending your time instead of spending your money can be incredibly profitable. So, along these lines, have you stopped to consider whether or not all of the things that you do for money are really worthwhile? Or are you just trading that time for someone else's time? We all have to keep a roof over our heads and keep the utilities on, but we don't have to have all of the little luxuries that the marketing industry strives to convince us are necessities.

If you make $20 an hour, think about how long you have to work to earn the following:

- Starbucks coffee: Fifteen minutes
- Dinner for four at a restaurant: Three hours
- Pre-made individual salads at the grocery store: Fifteen minutes
- Bathed dog: Three and a half hours

**A thrifty lifestyle is great for your family.**
By doing things for yourself, you can save a fortune every year. You can reduce your outgoing expenses to the point that you might have the freedom to have one parent stay at home with the kiddos. In turn, this can reduce your costs even more: suddenly there is no babysitter to pay and the at-home parent will have the time to do some of the other tasks for which you've previously had to pay for another person's time.

Not only does this reduce your expenses, it can also improve your quality of life dramatically. Suddenly you have time for garden-fresh produce, home-canned spaghetti sauce, and playing with the kids. You can teach your children how to grow and dry herbs, take them for walks to the library, and live the lesson that time is far more valuable than money. You can include them on the journey toward self-sufficiency and the reward is independent children who actually *know* their parents.

**A thrifty lifestyle can be much healthier.**
Many of the things that you do to save money are far healthier than the conveniences that you pay for. This is only true, of course, if you consciously choose the healthier option and not just the cheap option. A few positive health benefits might be:

- Growing an organic garden

- Foraging for wild nuts and berries
- Getting lots of exercise through your homesteading activities
- Making non-toxic cleaning supplies from everyday items like vinegar and orange peels
- Cooking from scratch and avoiding nasty additives and chemicals
- Walking a few blocks to the post office and library instead of driving
- Using non-toxic reusable containers instead of purchasing disposable items wrapped in BPA-containing plastic (an expense initially that saves you a lot in the long run)
- Preserving your own food instead of buying packaged food
- Doing your own yard work (exercise, fresh air)

Making these choices means that you suddenly have a lifestyle free of the toxic chemicals that most people are surrounded by.

**It teaches a self-sufficient mindset.**
Remember the old saying from the Depression?

*Use it up, wear it out, make it do, or do without*

That's like a creed in our house. We use the dish soap right down to the very last drop, then we add water, shake it up, and use that for a couple of days. Before we began making our own toothpaste, we'd actually cut open the tube that most folks would throw out and have an extra week of toothpaste we could scrape out. A basket sits in the living room beside a comfy chair containing all of the things that need to be mended, as well as the necessary repair supplies. (I can't be the only person who actually darns socks, can I?)

When I sit down with my family to watch a movie on Netflix, I like to do the mending. If there is nothing that requires repair, I like to make things, like dishcloths, rag rugs, or gifts. A lot can be done with an iron and some spray starch to make older clothes look crisp and new.

Most consumer goods today are designed with "planned obsolescence" in mind. I used to work in the automotive industry and learned that some vehicles are designed for a three- to four-year lifespan. At that point, components begin to fail and many consumers will then replace the vehicle with a newer model. The same is true with many other goods that you buy in the store. The mass manufacturers intend that you purchase a replacement in a few years. Items are not engineered with the potential for repair.

When making purchases, I would prefer to spend more money on a solidly made item with fewer plastic parts because I know it will last longer and that I will be able to either repair it myself or have it repaired if it breaks down. Defy the mass manufacturers by doing everything possible to repair an item before replacing it. And if it turns out that you *must* replace it, go for something of better quality if it is at all possible. Sometimes that better quality item might actually be an older item found at a thrift store or yard sale, because back in the day, planned obsolescence was not the goal of engineering like it is now.

Even better, don't replace it at all. If you can find a way to "do without" the item, you've won. For example, my home has a dryer, but I rarely use it. I got out of the habit in a previous home because my dryer broke and I didn't have the money to have it repaired or to replace it. I discovered that for a few dollars I could hang a clothesline and have fresh, crisp, air-dried laundry. What's more, it didn't run up my utility bills. Necessity bred a solution that was superior to the original situation.

I'm not much of a builder, but I've created relatively attractive bookcases using lumber that was kicking around the house and some sturdy boxes that I painted a nice color. When you think creatively, you'd be astonished at what you can create using what you already have on hand or can easily acquire from your environment. When you think you "need" something, take a day or two to consider how you might be able to repair, substitute or adapt. Often you will find that you didn't actually "need" that item in the first place.

### Save money by spending time.

The road to frugality is not earning more money, it's spending less. Saving money is far superior to earning it because the government can't tax what you don't earn or spend. A philosophy of personal thrift goes a long way toward "starving the beast."

# Part Six
## The Frugal Kitchen

There are many things that can happen which leave us without the ability to spend our usual grocery budget. But a lack of money doesn't mean that you don't still need to eat. In these cases, you'll need to shop for food with limited funds while still feeding your family tasty and nutritious meals.

### Flat-Broke Grocery Shopping

When your budget is super tight, grocery shopping is going to look a lot different. In my opinion, you're better off to shop for the entire month all at once when times are tough. Once-a-month shopping is a far less expensive way to purchase food, and I do it myself even when things aren't too bad.

When you are doing a flat-broke, once-a-month shopping trip, your diet may look a little different than it normally does. Remember, your goal is to get through the month without going hungry, not to go organic paleo. Don't plan on eating low-carb during a rough month. Unless, of course, you have a health condition that requires a low-carb diet, plan on adding more grains and starches to your diet during a rough spot. Also, you probably won't be able to eat organic. If you normally eat nothing but fresh, organic goodness, this month is going to have to be different. If times are really, really tight, you are going to need to loosen your standards to survive. If you are rock bottom broke, you may have to go even cheaper.

So, when I recommend canned fruits and lots of potatoes here in a minute, I don't want to hear "But according to your website, you're supposed to be the Organic Prepper." Sure. I am. But I'm also a sensible and realistic prepper. Just make the best choices you can while still staying fed, okay? Let's go through our food groups really quickly to give you an idea of what you'll be looking for on your shopping trip. None of these lists are comprehensive—you have to go with the things your family will eat and the things you can personally acquire inexpensively.

*Protein*
When you're broke, protein is going to be the costliest part of your menu.

**Meat:** When your budget is super tight, don't expect meat to be the main dish. I'm not saying you have to go vegetarian, but calorie for calorie, meat is very expensive. Use less meat than you normally would and make it an ingredient instead of the star of the meal. Go with less expensive cuts and cook them for a long time: stew beef, 70/30 ground beef, chicken quarters, chicken thighs, etc., are much less costly. You can also buy an inexpensive beef roast and an inexpensive whole chicken that will get you through several meals if carefully doled out.

**Eggs:** Eggs are a very inexpensive and healthy source of protein. Walmart has huge flats with thirty eggs for a very reasonable price. I suggest you grab a few of those and think about breakfast for dinner.

**Beans**: I absolutely love beans and strongly recommend them. Proper soaking and rinsing can reduce the resulting flatulence that a lot of folks worry about. Go with dried beans instead of canned for greater savings. (I'll explain how to cook them on page 117.) If your family members don't like beans, they might prefer refried beans or bean dip. Worst case scenario, you can puree cooked beans and add them to a soup for a nutrient boost.

**Peanut butter**: Peanut butter is a tasty protein source and most kids love it. (Assuming there are no allergies, of course.) Grab a huge jar and if possible, go for one that is more natural. Skippy and Jif both have a natural peanut butter without a whole lot of additives.

**Canned tuna:** Beware of eating this stuff non-stop because of high levels of mercury, but some canned tuna will add much-needed protein to your menu.

**Lentils and split peas:** Both of these are high in protein, dirt cheap, and easy to turn into delicious soups.

*Fruits and Vegetables*

Produce is a very important part of a healthy diet. Without it, you're at risk for all sorts of deficiency diseases. When shopping once a month, plan to eat your fresh stuff early in the month and then move on to your frozen or canned goods.

**Apples:** If the price is reasonable, grab a large bag of apples. This will provide you with some fresh fruit.

**Applesauce:** This is a great addition for later in the month when the fresh stuff is gone. To save money, look for large jars of applesauce instead of the little individual packets for lunch boxes. Go with unsweetened applesauce.

**Canned fruit:** Get fruit canned in the lightest syrup possible, or fruit canned in juice. Just because you're broke doesn't mean you need to eat ten pounds of sugar per day, right? Canned fruit is a nice addition to pancakes, waffles, or oatmeal. Reserve the juice for baking.

**Overripe bananas:** If your store has a last-day-of-sale bin for produce, you may be able to grab some overripe bananas. Get these and take them home for banana bread.

**Carrots:** I'm not talking about baby carrots here. I'm talking about those huge bags of grown-up carrots you'll need to peel and slice yourself. Remember earlier when I told you that you're either spending time or money? Carrots are a perfect example of that. Peel them, slice them, and keep them in a bowl of water in your fridge for yummy snacking.

**Potatoes:** A couple of bags of potatoes can get you through a rough time. Potatoes are filling, can be cooked in a lot of different ways, and most folks love them. Leave the peel on for added fiber. Store them in a cool, dark place away from onions for the longest life. Even when they're sprouting eyes, you can still eat them—just cut out the sprouting parts.

**Onions**: A big bag of onions will help you flavor up your home cooking this month.

**Garlic:** Sometimes it's cheaper to buy garlic already chopped up in a jar. Grab enough garlic to spice up your food over the course of the month.

**Cabbage:** Depending on the time of year, a few heads of cabbage will get you far for very little money. You can use cabbage in coleslaw, salads, soup, or casseroles. You don't need to get fancy—just go with the plain, ordinary green heads of cabbage if they're the cheapest.

**Canned tomatoes:** My favorite canned good is canned tomatoes. I like to get a variety of crushed and diced ones. These can be used for soups, chili, casseroles, and sauces. Canned tomatoes are a nutritional powerhouse.

**Frozen vegetables:** At my local grocery store, I can get bags of frozen vegetables for a dollar each, and sometimes less. If you have the freezer space, this is the way to go. I suggest you grab *at least* thirty bags of veggies that you know your family will enjoy. Our favorites are: peas and carrots, green peas, corn, cauliflower, broccoli, chopped spinach, Brussels sprouts, mixed vegetables, and green beans. With an assortment of frozen vegetables, you can make all sorts of great stuff.

**Whatever is in season**: Every season, there are fruits and veggies that are at their ripest and least expensive.

*Dairy*

If you consume dairy products on a daily basis, you're going to still want to consume dairy products when times are tough. (Cream for your coffee, milk for cereal, a beverage for the kiddos.) Generic milk by the gallon is your least expensive way to go for this. You can make all sorts of things from your gallons of milk, like homemade yogurt and cottage cheese. I suggest you put aside enough cash to be able to pick up a gallon of milk weekly. If you don't already have powdered milk, this isn't the time to buy it. It tends to be a lot more expensive than fresh milk.

Milk with lower fat can be frozen. Be sure to remove at least one cup of milk from your gallon jug to allow room for expansion. This works best with skim milk. Any milk with fat will need to be shaken each time you use it.

Grab cheese by the block for the least expensive option. Because we really enjoy cheese, I pick up two large blocks for a month. I cut each one in half and package them up separately. I freeze three and keep one in the fridge. Remember, cheese is *a condiment* during difficult times, not a main course. You simply cannot afford cheese and crackers for dinner.

*Grains*

I know this is a wildly unpopular ingredient these days, with all the low-carb and keto diets out there, but grains are the great stretchers of your pantry. You can take one serving of leftover chili and feed your entire family with it when you mix it with rice and a little bit of cheese.

Buy your grains in the biggest packages possible for the most savings. Forget about "instant" anything—these items are often totally stripped of nutrition, and again, you are spending time, or you are spending money. Here are some of the grains to look for:

- Brown rice
- Pasta
- Oats
- Quinoa
- Barley
- Flour
- Cornmeal

There are lots of other grains, but these are inexpensive, versatile, and easy to work with.

*Basics*

To turn your raw ingredients into meals, you'll need a few basics, too.

- Baking soda
- Baking powder
- Yeast (if you are going to bake bread)
- Spices
- Sugar, syrup, honey
- Fats (cooking oil, shortening, butter, lard, etc.)
- Vinegar
- Salt and pepper

**How much should you buy?**

This is the tricky part. How much to buy has a lot of variables and only you can identify them.

- What do you have on hand?

- How big is your family?
- How hungry is your family?
- How picky is your family?
- How long do you expect the budget to be tight?

The best option is to do some meal planning before you go shopping. This should help you identify how much you need for main meals. Don't forget to add extra for lunches and snacks!

## The "Whole Buffalo" Theory of Food Economics

In Native American lore, it is often said that hunters made use of the entire animal that they had killed in order to respect the sacrifice that sustained them. They considered the buffalo to be sacred, and felt it was an offense to be wasteful. They ate anything edible; they used the hides for shelters, shoes, and clothing; they strung bows with the sinews, they used the stomachs as water canteens, and they used the horns for weapons and tools.

One day years ago when I was preserving some peaches, my precocious homeschooled daughter pointed out that I was letting some parts go to waste. She said, "Mom, you need to use the whole buffalo!" So, I began to do some reading. I broke out all of my vintage cookbooks and began scouring the Internet and discovered that in this day and age, we sure do waste a lot of our buffalos. For many of us, budgets are tight. Whole, organic food is expensive, so in order to get our money's worth, we need to be creative and make it go as far as possible.

Back to peaches

Every summer, I get my hands on nearly 100 pounds of fresh, juicy peaches from a nearby orchard. That infamous year, my daughter pointed out that the pits and peels might be able to be used for something other than adding to our compost pile. So, here's what we did with the peaches:

- Jars of decadent vanilla-spiced peaches
- Jars of brown sugar peach preserves
- Jars of spicy peach jam
- Jars of sweet lemon peaches
- Peachsicles
- Peach peel candy (they taste a lot like gummy candies, but they aren't made of nasty chemical ingredients)
- Peach iced tea (from the pits)

- Peach vodka
- Jars of peach pit syrup

The only stuff that got tossed in the compost was the funky spots on the skin and the occasional mushy spot that we cut out and discarded. The only equipment we used was a water bath canner and a dehydrator.

### Growing food is sort of like having a baby.

When you put forth the effort to grow your own food, you realize how much work goes into it and you are far less likely to take it for granted. Sort of like carrying a baby around for nine months then pushing it out, you're going to take good care of anything that is that much work. (Okay, it's really not that much like having a baby, but go with my analogy—it's too much work to be careless with the results.)

When you shift to a more agrarian lifestyle, you begin to realize that although right now, there is so much more food than you could ever consume, that food won't be around forever. Berry season is fleeting, peaches are only here for a few short weeks, and tomatoes are in their glory only for the hottest part of the summer. If you want to put aside your local goodies, you are going to need to make the most of this bounty while it's here, or winter is going to be long and bland. Our ancestors managed fine without "fresh" blueberries and tomatoes in December, and with a little food preservation effort, you can too.

So, don't be shy about buying vast amounts of this-week's-yumminess at the farmers' market this weekend. With a little bit of research, you can make it go much further than one decadent meal. You even make some things last until next year!

### This is very budget friendly.

People ask me all the time how we can afford to eat an organic, local diet on a tight single mama budget. While it's true that the food we purchase often costs more than the food at the grocery store, the quality is so good that a simple slice of tomato is positively decadent. We actually find that we are far more satisfied with the delicious, chemical-free honest-to-goodness food that we eat. However, we still have to fill our tummies on more than a slice of tomato. That's why I go out of my way to find free food.

**There actually *is* such a thing as a free lunch.**

I have always considered anything you make from stuff that other people throw away to be free food. So, that free lunch? It consists of soup made from that chicken carcass that your family picked nearly clean at dinner last night, cooked along with those onion and veggie scraps that you kept in the freezer for the specific purpose of making a future soup. Most meals for a family of four cost between $10 to $20 when prepared at home, so if you make one free-bie meal a week, that will save you between $500 to $1,000 per year.

Snacks often cost $1 each when tucked into a lunch box, but if you make them from stuff most folks throw out (like peach peel candy) then it's free! So, if you can make five snacks a week for free, that will save you $260 over the course of the year.

I'm sure you see where I'm going with all of this. It just makes good economic sense to stretch your food as far as possible, while still eating nutritious, delicious wholesome ingredients.

**How else can you use the whole buffalo?**

Whatever you have in abundance, I can guarantee there are far more ways to use it than you have ever even thought about. Whether it is meat or produce, be willing to try some new things. For some of this, I thought back to my granny's kitchen and to the stories my dad told me about growing up during the Depression. For other stuff, I pored over old cookbooks and arcane websites.

This is just to get your wheels turning:

- **Watermelon:** Eat yummy fresh watermelon > dehydrate watermelon candy > make watermelon rind pickles
- **Pears:** Can pears > make pear peel butter > make juice or jam from the cores
- **Peaches:** Can peaches > dehydrate peach peel candy > make peach pit syrup > roast peach kernels
- **Chicken:** Roast a whole chicken > make a casserole or stir-fry > make broth from the carcass
- **Apples:** Can apple pie filling > make applesauce > make spiced apple cider-ish beverage from the cores

Once you've done all of this and you've made as many edible things as possible from your original item, you can still avoid the trash can. The fruit and vegetable by-products can be tossed onto the compost heap; the gristle from the meat can be made into dog treats (only in small amounts); and the bones can even be finely ground to make a bone meal soil amendment that also helps to frighten away "prey" animals like deer and rabbits.

Society has become so wasteful that many of these ideas may seem extreme. We live in a world of plenty, but that plenty comes at a grave cost. As a nation, our health is suffering, because "plenty" is a chemical concoction, first sealed in plastic and then in a cardboard box. What most people consider to be food is raised in horrible conditions in CAFOs or doused with toxic pesticides, then preserved with even more toxic chemicals. Everything is disposable, but no one thinks about where all of that "disposed" stuff goes. Our landfills are overflowing from the vast amounts of garbage that people throw away, and China no longer wants to take our trash. You'll find with the whole buffalo theory that you will end up with far less garbage and a much smaller grocery bill.

## Scratch Cooking Basics

If you compare the meals served in many of the kitchens today to meals served 100+ years ago, there is one very big difference. Nearly every meal served in North America has at least one dish that has come from a box, bag, or pouch. Take breakfast, for example. Did you have toast? If so, did you make the bread? Cereal? One of those little packs of Quaker oatmeal, all flavored up and just waiting for you to add water? Did your breakfast originate in the freezer? Frozen toaster versions of pancakes, waffles, and pastries abound in many kitchens.

In a world that is ever-increasingly geared toward convenience, few people take the time to roll out noodles or bake cookies these days. Birthday cakes come from the bakery, cookies come from a bag with a convenient tab to reseal it, and bread comes from a shelf at the grocery store, so perfectly uniform that if you put it back and mixed all the loaves up, you'd never find the original loaf. (Anyone who has ever baked a loaf of bread will tell you, they all get a funny lump here and there!)

All of this easy-access food has taken a deeper toll than you might imagine.

. . . A toll on our health.

. . . A toll on our waistlines.

. . . A toll on our ability to make even the simplest item on our own.

. . . A toll on the time we spend with our families.

. . . A toll on the next generation, when we fail to teach them the arts that are vanishing as our grandparents pass away.

Cooking from scratch is actually an analogy for today's society. Taking the road less traveled is considered an eccentric throwback to a faraway time. People feel that we are making unnecessary work for ourselves and that our lives would be vastly improved by tossing a shiny cellophane bag of bread into the grocery cart instead of taking a couple of hours to mix the ingredients, knead the dough, let it rise, knead it some more, then shape it into the desired form.

But when you toss that bag of bread into the cart, you are paying for someone else's time spent to make that bread. You are getting undesirable ingredients. You are missing out on teaching your child how to judge the composition of the dough by the feel of it in her hands when she kneads it. You don't get to inhale that delicious aroma emanating from your oven, and you totally skip that mouth-watering anticipation as you let the loaf rest long enough for you to slice it. Packaged bread from the store doesn't serve as so fine a vehicle for melting fresh butter and transferring it your mouth as when you finally get to cut into your fresh, wholesome bread.

### Scratch cooking is easier than it seems.

The media is partly to blame for making it seem difficult to actually cook. Most of the advertisements for processed food available at the grocery store tout the convenience of these items. You never see a mom with flour all over the front of her apron and her hair in a ponytail. Instead, the TV-commercial mothers are perfectly coiffed, wearing high heels and a skirt, placing a dish on the table with a flawlessly manicured hand. They are never rushed or harried, of course, because they've used pre-shredded cheese along with their premade noodles and can of sauce. They look like they just stepped out of the office and, "poof," a dinner has appeared in their kitchens.

If you can read and possess the ability to use a measuring cup, you can cook. It's that simple. It seems almost fashionable lately to claim an inability to cook, as though preparing food is beneath a certain level of sophistication. When you start out, sure, there is some trial and error. Sometimes you end up having a peanut butter sandwich in the early years. But for the most part, with some very basic tools, cooking is foolproof.

Case in point: my oldest daughter was a little bit behind on reading when she was in 3rd grade. However, she had a fascination with cooking. So, to help improve her reading skills, I began letting her cook. She would pore through my cookbooks and choose a meal. She'd make a list, then we'd check what we had in the house and what we needed from the store. When she was nine years old, she made a cheese lasagna, from scratch, including the marinara sauce, completely unaided. (And it was delicious!) Basic scratch cooking is not some mysterious art that requires four years at Le Cordon Bleu in Paris—it's just a simple matter of reading instructions and putting them into action.

**It doesn't take that much additional time.**

The thing is, with a bit of pre-planning, even the busiest working mother can cook from scratch, without the use of convenience items. Every weekend I spend a few hours in the kitchen prepping food for the week ahead. I do some baking (cookies, granola bars, and bread), clean and chop up veggies, pack little containers of healthy snacks for my daughter's lunch, and cook a few items to be used throughout the week. I usually roast something on the week-end and cook up some seasoned ground beef or turkey, then add these things to meals throughout the week. I was more focused on this when I worked outside the home, but still do it to some degree.

Never forget about your crockpot! That valuable kitchen appliance can have dinner ready and waiting when you get home from a long day at the office, in the garden, or out with the kiddos. It makes delicious pot roasts and even rotisserie-style chicken! It's also great for soups, stews, chili, and spaghetti sauce. You can make the cheapest cut of meat tender and delicious by slow-cooking it for ten hours on low, so this is helpful to the budget as well.

**It's healthier.**

Any item you make from scratch is going to be far healthier than its convenience food equivalent. Take cookies, for example. Who doesn't love cookies? I bake them two to three times per week—there are always some in the jar. However, the ones I make at home contain wholesome ingredients like freshly ground flour, organic sugar, coconut oil, and dried fruit. The ones that I would buy at the grocery store, nine times out of ten, would contain unsavory ingredients that we wish to avoid. When you make it yourself, you know precisely what is in it. You know that your family member with allergies is safe, that you aren't unknowingly using artificial ingredients, and that you aren't ingesting preservatives that do double duty as drain cleaner.

### It's cheaper.

Now for the part every self-respecting Frugalite loves. You will save a *ton* of money cooking it yourself. For example, a one-cup serving of brown rice, cooked in broth and prepared from scratch, costs less than 10 cents (and contains nothing yucky). A one-cup serving of flavored Uncle You-Know-Who's rice costs up to $1. A cup of oatmeal from bulk-purchased steel-cut oats costs about 5 cents, but a little brown packet that you pour boiling water over costs 50 cents.

The reason for this? Time is money. Whether it's your time or the food manufacturer's time, there is a cost involved. Some people feel that it's worth it to pay for this convenience. What they don't consider is that the hands-on time in cooking these items from scratch is often minimal. For example, I use the oven to bake my brown rice and all I have to do is bring the pot to a boil on the stove top, put it in the oven for 1 hour, and walk away. If that hour is not "hands-on time," then I really don't think it could be considered an hour of actual work, do you?

Shopping to stock your pantry and purchasing basic items in bulk will save you a fortune at the grocery store. As an added bonus, you'll find that by keeping a good supply of all your basic items, you will end up having to make fewer trips to the grocery store. (And come on, every time you go to the store, if you're anything like me, you end up with at least *one* thing that wasn't on your list! Right?)

### Here's how to get started with scratch cooking.

The first thing you need to do is acquire a good cookbook. I have lots of cookbooks that have been purchased at yard sales and library sales over the years. I find that the most valuable, the ones I turn to again and again, are the old books. I really love cookbooks that were written during the Great Depression, or even earlier.

My prized possession is my Fannie Farmer cookbook, written in 1896 and originally published as *The Boston Cooking-School Cookbook*. I have referred to this book again and again because it has instructions for things that are rather difficult to find in more modern tomes. As well, you don't find ingredients like canned "cream of whatever" soup—you are walked through making a basic béchamel sauce instead.

With the Internet, you can find basic instructions for making just about anything. Find an author that doesn't use hard-to-find ingredients and that shows step-by-step illustrations. I really love the Martha Stewart website for the clarity of the instructions, but Martha is in a rather different economic bracket and sometimes her recipes contain very pricey ingredients. Her 101 articles can't be beaten, though.

Next, be sure you have some basic kitchen supplies. You need basic cookware and utensils, obviously. Other useful (but not 100 percent necessary) items are:

- Kitchen timer (this is very, very important unless your attention span is far more keen than mine)
- Inexpensive little food processor
- Instant-read thermometer (more important when you're just starting out—with experience you will be able to judge when something is the "right" temperature)
- Good, sharp knife
- Box grater with different sized holes
- Set of measuring cups and spoons
- Colander
- Whisk
- Potato masher
- Crockpot

I'm not a huge fan of gadgets, particularly electric ones. They are expensive, they break down, and then they need to be replaced.

## Experiment!

Once you have the basics down, you can begin to experiment, and this is what separates the "decent" cooks from the really "great" cooks. Initially, don't veer too far from the original recipe. You can start by altering the spices to suit the preferences of your family. Next thing you know, you'll look at a recipe, get a general idea of what they're making, and then set off to create your own unique dish!

Learning a few scratch cooking basics can really help you out when times are tight. Remember—with just about anything you eat, either you're spending time or you're spending money to pay for someone else's time. If your budget is super-tight, then you're going to need to spend time. The next section is filled with simple instructions for scratch cooking basics to get you started.

## How to Bake Rice

When purchasing rice, brown rice is the best choice. It has more fiber and more nutrients than white rice. Some folks avoid brown rice because they think it's difficult to cook. Take it off of the stovetop and cook it in the oven for absolutely perfect rice every time. For efficiency, bake your rice when you are cooking something else in the oven.

### Ingredients:

- 1½ cups brown rice
- 2½ cups water, broth, or stock
- Salt, pepper, and herbs to taste
- 1 tbsp butter or olive oil

### Directions:

1. Preheat the oven to 400°F.
2. On the stovetop, bring rice, liquid, seasonings, and fat to a boil in an oven-safe pot.
3. Immediately put the lid on it, remove it from the stovetop, and place it in the oven.
4. Bake for 1 hour. Do not remove the lid during the cooking time.
5. Fluff the rice with a fork and serve immediately.

Leftover rice can be refrigerated and used in a casserole or stir-fry. In fact, I suggest you make a *huge* batch of it to use in other recipes and meals throughout the week.

## How to Cook Dried Beans

There are minor differences in soaking and cooking times with different types of beans, but if you follow these basic directions, you'll be successful. The obvious, common sense difference is that smaller beans require a shorter cooking time than larger beans.

Prepping the beans for cooking:

- Start with one pound of dried beans. My favorites are pinto beans and navy beans.
- Pour them into a bowl and pick through them, discarding any beans that are dry and shriveled, and any little stones or twigs.
- Using a large colander, rinse the beans well under running water.

- Place your beans in a large stockpot. Cover them with water by 3 to 4 inches.
- Turn the stove on high and bring the beans to a boil. Turn off the heat immediately and soak them, covered. You can soak them overnight, or a minimum of four hours.
- Drain the beans using a colander, then rinse them well under running water.

**Directions:**
1. Return the soaked beans to the stockpot.
2. Cover them with 6 cups of water per 2 cups of beans.
3. If you want, you can also add some meat at this point. Salt pork, ham, and bacon are popular choices. If you aren't using meat, add 1 tablespoon of vegetable oil. The fat not only adds flavor but keeps the beans from foaming.
4. You can also add onions, garlic, and herbs to the beans now. Don't add anything acidic until they are fully cooked.
5. Bring the beans to a boil, then immediately reduce the heat to keep them at a simmer.
6. Stir occasionally to be sure the beans aren't sticking. The beans must always stay covered with water. You may need to add water during the cooking process.
7. Simmer for 2 to 3 hours. To test whether they are done, remove a bean from the pot and let it cool. Taste it—it should be tender, but not mushy. There are lots of variables that will affect how long they take to cook—weather conditions, altitude, and the age of the beans can affect cooking times.

When they're done, you can leave them in the cooking liquid or drain them, based on personal preferences. (I grew up down south, where my family always enjoyed them in the "bean broth.")

**How to Make One-Pot Beans and Rice**
Beans and rice are the king and queen of cheap eats. And with the right seasoning, they're good too!

**Ingredients:**
- 1 cup dried beans

- 6 cups water
- 2 cups brown rice

**Seasoning options:**
- Cumin, chili powder, garlic powder, and onion powder
- Cajun seasoning mix
- Garlic, onion, thyme, and sage
- Bay leaf, tomato paste, and paprika

**Directions:**
1. Rinse and sort through dried beans, discarding any that aren't good.
2. Soak the beans in the fridge overnight.
3. In the morning, drain the beans and rinse them. Then add them to your pot and bring them to a simmer for 1 hour.
4. Add the brown rice and seasonings into the pot and cook for 1 more hour.
5. Taste test to make sure both the beans and the rice are fully cooked and tender.

**How to Make Gravy**

There are two kinds of gravy, at least if you're from the south. This is how to make a simple brown gravy.

**Ingredients:**
- 2 tbsp meat drippings
- 3 tbsp flour
- 2 cups broth, drippings, or water
- Salt and pepper to taste

**Directions:**
1. Add meat drippings to a saucepan and turn the heat on your stove to medium.
2. When the drippings are hot enough that a tiny bit of water splashed into the skillet off your fingertips sizzles on contact, use a whisk to mix in 2 tbsp flour. Whisk vigorously until the flour and fat are completely incorporated with no lumps. You should end up with a smooth, creamy looking mixture. (This is called a roux.)
3. Stir in the water or broth. Broth gives a slightly richer flavor, but gravy made with water is still delicious and much more frugal. Using the whisk, mix the roux and water thoroughly.

4. Cook, whisking almost continuously, for 3 to 5 minutes until your gravy reaches a uniform consistency and the desired thickness. If it is too thick, whisk in more liquid, ½ cup at a time.
5. Keep warm over the lowest heat your stove allows.
6. Season with salt and pepper to taste.

Gravy *rocks* because it can make a lesser cut of meat taste delicious. Your gravy leftovers (if you have any) can be used as the basis of a nice soup or stew.

**How to Make Yogurt**
Homemade yogurt is tangy enough to use in place of sour cream on potatoes or in recipes. Making it yourself is a fraction of the price of store-bought yogurt. You control the level of fat in your yogurt by the milk you choose. Not only is homemade yogurt healthier than store-bought, it's much less expensive, particularly if you prefer to give your family organic or raw dairy products. Note: This recipe will work with any type of dairy milk but will not work with non-dairy milk.

Here's the math:

One gallon of milk makes approximately two quarts of yogurt.

- One gallon of organic milk is $6.99 from our local Safeway.
- One quart of organic yogurt is $4.99.
- By making our own yogurt, using a little of a previous batch to start the new batch, the cost per quart is only $3.50.

Something I strongly recommend for your preparedness supplies is some freeze-dried yogurt starter. If disaster strikes, you won't be able to run to the store to get a small container of yogurt to start a batch, so this is great to have on hand. It is definitely more expensive than using ready-made yogurt as a starter, but it's a great way to extend the life of milk in a down-grid scenario.

It's easy to make yogurt at home. The only issue for some folks is that it is time-consuming. While it does take time, it isn't all hands-on time. You have to be near the stove to watch the temperature of the milk. Because of this, I usually start my milk as we're finishing up dinner, then finish the process as I'm cleaning up the kitchen for the day. Since I'm going to be in the kitchen for an hour then anyway, it doesn't seem like I'm spending a huge amount of time making yogurt.

There are cool little yogurt-making machines that you can buy for a very reasonable price—less than $30. But you don't have to have a machine to make yogurt. I'm going to tell you about two very simple methods for making yogurt. You can go off-grid and make it in a thermos, or for larger batches, you can use your dehydrator.

The first steps are the same for both methods. (Actually, the first steps are the same if you have a yogurt-making machine too.) Here's what you need:

- ½ gallon (2 quarts) milk
- Culture: ¼–½ cup organic full-fat yogurt or 2 packets freeze-dried starter
- Food thermometer (I absolutely love my digital instant read thermometer.)

That's it!

### Directions:

1. In a large saucepan, gently bring the milk up to 165°F. Some people, when using raw milk, raise the temperature only to 120°F so that they don't pasteurize the milk. (However, when you turn the milk into yogurt, you'll be adding in healthy bacteria, so this is entirely optional.)
2. When your milk reaches the desired temperature, remove it from the heat and allow it to cool. Be sure to remove it from the element if you have an electric stove or it will continue to get hotter. If you go over 185°F, your yogurt may not turn out well.
3. Allow your milk to cool to anywhere between 108°F and 112°F. If it is any hotter than that when you mix it with the culture, you'll kill the bacteria that turn the milk into yogurt. If it is cooler, then it won't be warm enough for the culturing process to occur. (This specifically is why I recommend a digital instant read thermometer.)
4. When the milk drops to the desired temperature, ladle out about 1 cup of it to mix in another bowl with your culture. (This can be yogurt from the store, yogurt from a previous batch, or a freeze-dried starter.) Whisk it gently to combine it thoroughly. You're not making whipped cream or meringue.
5. Pour the mixture back into the pot with the rest of the milk and whisk gently to combine it well.

This is where the paths of yogurt-making diverge, but read all the way to the end, because the paths merge again.

**The Thermos Method:** This is an off-grid way to make yogurt. It's useful because it adds to the lifespan of your milk if the power goes out. I generally use this method because it uses no power and I like to be thrifty. Use a good quality, large thermos for this. Don't use one of those little-kid, plastic lunch box thermoses. A thermos is a good thing to have around in a down-grid scenario, so you'll find this to be a multipurpose item.

- While you're prepping your yogurt, fill your thermos with hot water so that the temperature inside it is nice and warm when you pour in the mixture. If the mixture cools down too quickly from meeting the chilled walls of the thermos, your yogurt will not turn out.
- Empty the thermos, reserving the water for some other use.
- Pour or ladle the mixture from the pot into the thermos. Use a funnel to help guide the milk into the thermos.
- Put the lid on the thermos immediately.
- Leave the thermos in the warmest place in the house overnight. For us, this is the laundry room at our current home. At another home, we tucked the thermos behind the woodstove.
- Allow your yogurt to culture in the thermos for 10 to 14 hours. The longer you leave it, the more tart it will be.

(You're not quite done. Be sure to skip down to the "Last Steps" section.)

**The Dehydrator Method:** This method can be used if you have one of those nice large dehydrators with removable trays like the Excalibur. It must have removable trays and temperature settings for this to work. If you are going out and buying a dehydrator specifically for the purpose of making yogurt, it would be much better to get the yogurt-making machine instead. And by better, I mean $200 cheaper. However, if you already have an Excalibur or similar dehydrator, this is just one more use for it.

- Heat up enough Mason jars to hold all of the milk you're preparing by filling them with hot water and setting the lids on top of them.

- Remove the shelves from your dehydrator and begin preheating it to 105°F.
- When your milk has been mixed with the culture, empty the water from the jars.
- Using a canning funnel, fill the jars with the yogurt-to-be, leaving 1 inch of headspace.
- Place the lid on the jars. (I use old lids that have previously been canned with for this, since I don't need a seal.)
- Place the jars in your dehydrator and close it. Leave the temperature at 105°F and allow the jars to stay in for 10 to 12 hours. (Some instructions say 8 hours, but my yogurt was watery when I did that.) The longer the yogurt stays in the warmth, the more tart it will be.

You're not quite done . . . read on.

**Last Steps:** When you make homemade yogurt, it isn't immediately going to have the super-thick texture that you get with store bought yogurt. Some people stir in a thickener like unflavored gelatin. When you do this, you have the goodness of the whey and you don't have to take the extra steps of draining it. However, I prefer to drain my yogurt and use the whey for other purposes.

- Place a large colander in a larger bowl.
- Line the colander with a lint free, clean dish towel.
- Pour the yogurt into your draining set up. It will be very liquid-y but don't despair!
- Drain the yogurt for at least 2 hours. The longer you drain it, of course, the thicker the yogurt will be. I like to pull mine when it is the texture of sour cream, but if you leave it overnight, it will be the delicious thick consistency of cream cheese.

Ridiculously easy, right? The longer you leave it, the thicker and more tart your yogurt will be. If you intend to use it in place of sour cream, leave it longer. Always save a little of your yogurt to be a starter for the next batch. I like to put ½ cup in the fridge, stored separately so it doesn't accidentally get eaten.

### How to Make Cottage Cheese

You can make this creamy deliciousness with only three simple ingredients:

#### Ingredients:
- 2½ cups 2% milk
- ¼ cup white vinegar
- Dash of salt (optional—it's just for flavor)

#### Directions:
1. In a large saucepan bring the milk almost to a boil. As soon as bubbles begin to rise to the top, remove the saucepan from the heat.
2. Immediately stir in the white vinegar and the salt (if using). The milk will begin to curdle right away.
3. Allow the mixture to cool completely—about 1 hour at room temperature. (The longer you leave it to cool, the more curds you will have. You can even put it in the fridge overnight before draining.)
4. Using a mesh strainer, separate the curds and the whey. (Hints of Little Miss Muffet!)

The result will be a delicious, light, and fluffy cottage cheese. This recipe falls just short of 1 cup of cottage cheese and just over 1½ cups of whey. If the flavor is a bit sour you can rinse the curds gently under running water, then drain again.

Don't throw out your whey!
Here are some uses for it:

- Substitute for water or milk in baking
- Use instead of water when cooking rice or pasta
- Use it for smoothies
- Use it in oatmeal or other porridge

### How to Make Homemade Coffee Creamer

Coffee creamer is delicious. It's not necessarily the healthiest or the most budget-friendly addition to your cuppa joe, however. And fun fact: a lot of them don't even contain cream! It's incredibly easy to make your own coffee creamer, and it's a fraction of the price of those store-bought chemistry projects.

**Sweet Cream:** Sweet cream is very basic—it's simply your dairy or dairy alternative, warmed enough to dissolve your sweetener. The joy of this recipe is that you can use any kind of dairy or dairy alternative and any kind of sweetener. I'm old school and use half-and-half with brown sugar.

Other options include animal product alternatives like soy milk, rice milk, and nut milk. For sweetener, you can use any kind of sugar, stevia, or agave nectar. Honey is always a delicious and healthy option to sweeten anything.

### Base ingredients:
- 1½ cups milk of your choice
- 1½ cups milk or cream of your choice
- 4 tbsp sugar or flavors (suggestions below)

### Directions:
1. Bring 1½ cups of milk and 1½ cups of cream (or your milk of choice) to a low simmer.
2. Mix the sugar or flavoring into the milk and bring to a simmer on the stove, whisking constantly until it begins to steam slightly.
3. Remove from heat, allow to cool, then store in the refrigerator. Feel free to adjust the amounts for stronger or sweeter flavors. Don't bring it to a boil, because your creamer will curdle.

### Flavors:
If you have a passion for fancy coffee flavors, here are some inexpensive ideas for tweaking your homemade creamer.

- **Mocha Java:** 2 tbsp cocoa powder, 4 tbsp brown sugar
- **Mexican Mocha Java:** 2 tbsp cocoa powder, 4 tbsp brown sugar, 1 tsp cinnamon
- **Nutella *aka* Chocolate Hazelnut:** 4 tbsp Nutella—no other sweetener needed
- **Gingerbread:** 2 tsp molasses, 2 tbsp brown sugar, ½ tsp each of ginger, clove, and cinnamon
- **Almond Toffee:** 4 tbsp brown sugar, 1 tsp almond extract
- **Vanilla Latte:** 2 teaspoons pure vanilla extract, 4 tbsp white sugar
- **Great White North Maple Java:** 6 tbsp pure maple syrup

- **Mocha Mint:** 2 tbsp cocoa powder, ½ tsp pure peppermint extract, 4 tbsp white sugar
- **Cinnamon Roll:** 2 tsp cinnamon, 1 tsp vanilla extract, 4 tbsp brown sugar, and a dash of salt (yep, salt)
- **Caramel Macchiato:** 6 tbsp brown sugar, a dash of salt, 1 tbsp cocoa, and ½ tsp pure vanilla extract
- **Cherry Amaretto:** 1 tbsp almond extract, 4 tbsp white sugar, ½ tsp cherry extract
- **White Chocolate Mocha:** 1 cup white chocolate chips, 1 tsp cocoa (melt the chips into the milk, whisking constantly)
- **Mint White Chocolate:** 1 cup white chocolate chips, 1 tsp pure peppermint extract
- **Black Forest:** 2 tbsp cocoa, 4 tbsp brown sugar, 1 tsp cherry extract
- **Chocolate Coconut Mocha:** 2 tbsp cocoa, 4 tbsp white sugar, 2 tsp coconut extract (or replace half of the milk with coconut milk)
- **Irish Cream:** 2 tbsp cocoa, 1 tsp pure vanilla extract, ½ tsp almond extract, 2 tbsp instant coffee, 4 tbsp white sugar
- **Eggnog:** 1 tsp pure vanilla extract, 2 tsp rum extract, 1 tsp nutmeg
- **Pumpkin Pie Latte:** 3 tbsp pumpkin puree, 1 tsp pumpkin pie spice, 1 tsp cinnamon, 4 tbsp brown sugar, 1 teaspoon vanilla extract
- **Hazelnut:** 1 tsp hazelnut extract, 1 tsp pure vanilla extract, 4 tbsp white sugar
- **Frangelico Cream:** 1 tbsp cocoa, 1 tsp hazelnut extract, 1 tsp pure vanilla extract, and 4 tbsp brown sugar
- **Chai Latte:** Simmer 3 chai tea bags in creamer mixture with 4 tbsp brown sugar
- **Chocolate Raspberry:** 4 tbsp seedless raspberry jelly, 2 tbsp cocoa
- **Almond Joy:** 2 tbsp cocoa, 4 tbsp white sugar, 1 tsp almond extract, and 2 tsp coconut extract (or replace half of the milk with coconut milk)
- **Salted Caramel:** 6 tbsp brown sugar, a dash of salt

If you want to be extra fancy, top it off with a dollop of whipped cream and a sprinkle of cocoa or cinnamon powder.

### How to Make Corn Bread

This quick bread was a staple when I was growing up. My dad, who was a child of the Great Depression, loved nothing more than a big slice of corn bread topped with pinto beans in their own broth. Unless perhaps it was corn bread broken up into a glass of buttermilk and eaten with a spoon, a dish I never personally enjoyed.

Some people like their corn bread sweet, while others don't like the addition of any sugar or honey. This ingredient is entirely optional. This recipe is naturally gluten free, so it doesn't rise much. If you want a fluffy corn bread, replace half of the cornmeal with flour. Maybe I'm a traditionalist, but in my humble opinion, corn bread is at its best when cooked in a cast-iron skillet.

### Ingredients:

- 1 tbsp white vinegar
- 1½ cups milk
- 4 tbsp butter or cooking oil + extra for greasing your skillet
- 2 cups cornmeal
- 1 tsp salt
- 1 tsp baking soda
- 2 tsp baking powder
- 4 tbsp brown sugar or honey (optional)
- 1 egg

### Directions:

1. Preheat the oven to 400°F.
2. In a bowl, mix white vinegar and milk and set it aside for at least 5 minutes to allow it to sour.
3. Grease the skillet well with oil or butter.
4. Meanwhile, in a large mixing bowl, combine the cornmeal, salt, baking soda, baking powder, and sugar (if you are using it) with a whisk.
5. Add eggs and honey (if you're using it) to the sour milk. Whisk until well-combined.
6. Stir the wet ingredients into the dry ingredients until they are just combined.
7. Pour this mixture into the cast-iron skillet.
8. Bake the corn bread for about 20 minutes. The top should be golden brown and crispy, and a toothpick inserted in the middle should come out clean.

**Corn Bread Variations:**
**Mexican Corn Bread:** Add 1 cup of cooked corn, a couple of diced jalapeños, and a cup of shredded cheese to the batter. Reduce the sweetener by half.

**Blueberry Corn Bread:** Add 1 cup of fresh, frozen, or rehydrated blueberries to the corn bread batter. Sugar and honey should definitely be used when making blueberry corn bread.

## How to Make a Roux

This white sauce is a thrifty and inexpensive basis for casseroles or anything that calls for a can of cream-of-whatever soup.

### Ingredients:
- 2 tbsp butter
- 2 tbsp flour
- 2 cups milk (or 1 cup milk + 1 cup water)
- Salt, pepper, and appropriate seasonings

### Directions:
1. Melt the butter in a skillet, and then whisk in the flour.
2. Let it thicken up for a moment, then stir in 1 cup milk, whisking constantly.
3. Once this has thickened up, add the second cup of liquid and the seasonings.
4. Reduce the heat and stir every couple of minutes for five minutes.

Use your white sauce in your recipe or add some Parmesan cheese and garlic to make a simple Alfredo sauce for pasta or rice.

## How to Make Pie Crust

Pie crust isn't just for dessert. (See the "Leftover Magic" section on page 135 for savory pie crust ideas.) The beauty of my granny's pie crust recipe is the versatility—you can use what you have. Ideally, I use butter and water for the fat and liquid. However, I have used many different ingredients with excellent results. This recipe makes enough for one double-crust pie or two single-crust pies.

**Ingredients:**
- ½ cup liquid (water, milk, or whey)
- 3 cups flour
- 2 tsp salt
- 1 cup fat (butter, shortening, coconut oil, lard, or vegetable oil)

**Directions:**
1. Place your liquid in a dish with a few pieces of ice, if available. Keep this in the refrigerator while you're combining the other ingredients.
2. Combine the flour and salt.
3. Cut the butter or fat into tiny pieces and incorporate it into the flour mixture, either with a pastry cutter, a food processor, or a couple of knives. Once the mixture resembles cottage cheese curds, you have combined it sufficiently.
4. Add your ice water to the mixture a couple of tablespoons at a time. This is where practice makes perfect—after you make this a couple of times, you will begin to know when it looks and feels "right." Use a fork to mix this into the dough—if you use your hands you will heat up the dough too much and the crust won't be as flaky.
5. You don't want the dough to be wet and sticky—you want it to be sort of stringy and lumpy. When you think you have the right consistency, squeeze some dough in your hand—if it stays into a nice firm ball, it's time to move on to the next step. If it is crumbly and doesn't stick together, you need more water.
6. Make the dough into 2 balls and press them down. Place them, covered, in the refrigerator for at least 1 hour.
7. On a floured surface, roll out the dough with a heavy rolling pin until it is thin but not broken. Fold your circle of dough into quarters and carefully move the dough over to your pie pan.
8. Bake at about 375°F for approximately 45 minutes for a two-crust pie or 35 minutes for a one-crust pie.

## How to Make Frugalite Pizza

Pizza is my life. I'm sorry, I know it isn't glamorous, but put it on crust and top it with cheese and it's an instant hit with my family. Sometimes I go all out and spend a while making a delicious homemade pizza dough from scratch. (It's the next recipe.) It's so incredibly good and the house smells even better.

But I don't always have the time or inclination to do the big hurrah. When that's the case and we need a super-quick yet satisfying meal on the table, I make Frugalite pizzas. There's a secret ingredient for Frugalite pizza: flour tortillas.

What?

Yes, flour tortillas. If you don't do gluten, you can obviously use gluten-free tortillas. When prepared with a tortilla crust, the result is a light, crisp, thin crust pizza.

### Directions:
1. Preheat your oven to 400°F.
2. Brush the cookie sheet with cooking oil.
3. Prep your pizzas right on the cookie sheet.
4. Bake them for about 5 to 10 minutes. Check them frequently once you reach the 5-minute mark to make sure the crust is how you like it.

### What should you put on Frugalite Pizza?
Here are five of our favorite ideas for your frugal pizza night.

**Classic:** Use your favorite pizza toppings, like marinara sauce, pepperoni, mushrooms, olives, peppers, or whatever floats your boat. Top it with mozzarella cheese.

**Leftover:** Use whatever sauce goes with your toppings, like marinara or alfredo. Top the pizza with your leftover meat from the night before, like shredded chicken, thin-sliced steak, chopped ham, crumbled hamburger, or sliced sausage. Roasted vegetables are a delicious addition. Add some veggies from the fridge and top it with an appropriate cheese.

**BBQ:** Instead of marinara sauce, spread barbecue sauce on the tortilla. Top this with cooked chicken (or beef or whatever), and veggies like onions and peppers, then cover the whole delicious thing with cheddar or provolone.

**Fiesta:** Spread the tortilla with refried beans, then top it with ground beef (if wanted), salsa, or fresh tomatoes and peppers. Sprinkle cheddar cheese on top. Dip a dollop of sour cream and guacamole on top when it's done.

**Buffet:** Let everyone top their own pizzas with the goodies that you have frugally dished out for them to choose from. Top with their favorite pizza additions and either marinara or BBQ sauce, and cheese. If you have overly enthusiastic family members, dish out their cheese yourself.

### How to Make Delicious Pizza Dough

After the dough has risen, you can have some delicious homemade pizza faster than you can say "Domino's."

#### Ingredients:
- 1 cup warm water
- 1 tbsp sugar
- 2¼ tsp active dry yeast
- 3 tbsp olive oil
- 1 tsp salt
- 2½–3 cups flour

#### Directions:
1. Stir water, sugar, and yeast together and allow it to sit for 5 minutes.
2. Add olive oil and salt, then stir in the flour until well blended.
3. Knead the dough for about 5 minutes, then let it rise, covered, for 30 minutes.
4. Preheat the oven to 425°F.

#### To make pizza:
1. Knead the dough again, then roll it out and place it on your pizza pan.
2. Add your toppings.
3. Bake the pizza at 425°F for 20 to 25 minutes until the crust is done and the cheese is melted.

#### To make pockets:
1. Knead the dough again, then break off balls of dough. Roll them out and cover half with the desired topping.
2. Fold the other half over the topping, moisten the edges with water, and press them together with the tines of a fork.
3. Place the pocket on a greased baking sheet.

4.  Once all the pockets are on the baking sheet, brush them lightly with olive oil. If desired, season the top with a sprinkle of garlic powder and salt, or whatever herbs are appropriate.
5.  Bake for 20 to 25 minutes, or until lightly golden brown.

### How to Make Multipurpose Biscuit Dough

This recipe can be used for biscuits—simply bake for 10 to 15 minutes. As well, you can roll this dough out and cut it into thin strips, dropping it into boiling broth until it floats to the top (7 to 10 minutes) to make dumplings.

#### Ingredients:

*   ½ cup milk
*   1 tbsp white vinegar
*   2 cups flour
*   3 tsp baking powder
*   1 tsp sugar
*   1 tsp salt
*   3 tbsp cooking oil

#### Directions:

1.  Preheat oven to 425°F.
2.  Mix milk and vinegar in a small bowl and allow it to sit for about 5 minutes.
3.  Mix flour, baking powder, sugar, and salt in a bowl. Add milk and vinegar mixture, and oil.
4.  Stir just enough to hold dough together.
5.  Knead lightly about 10 times on a well-floured surface.
6.  Pat or roll dough about ½-inch thick.
7.  You can move the dough in one piece over to your pie pan or you can cut circles with a floured drinking glass and place the individual biscuits on the dish you are topping.
8.  Bake for 15 to 20 minutes or until golden brown. Top with butter if desired.

### How to Make Bone Broth

The health benefits of bone broth have been talked about a lot recently, but the cost of buying it at the store is expensive. The good news is, it's very easy and inexpensive to make it from scratch. Bone broth has been tied to improvements in:

- Gut health
- Joint pain from arthritis or other issues
- Boosting your immune system

It helps with all of these things because it provides easily bioavailable nutrients like:

- Calcium
- Magnesium
- Phosphorus
- Silicon
- Sulphur
- Chondroitin Sulfate
- Glucosamine
- Gelatin
- Collagen
- Amino Acids

You can make bone broth from any type of bones, but the most popular are chicken, turkey, beef, and lamb. I usually make my broth in the crockpot, where you can assemble it and then forget about it for the next day or two (aside from the glorious smells)!

While you don't have to add anything except your bones and water, I like to add fresh garlic and onion for the added benefits. For best results, get the highest quality bones you can find—preferably grass-fed, free range, and organic. Avoid anything that has been treated with antibiotics or hormones. Use any bones you have left over from a meal, or purchase marrow bones from a butcher.

**Directions:**
1. Place the bones into the crockpot. It's fine if they have some meat on them.
2. Add any other stuff you want in the broth, like garlic and onion. Some people like to add bay leaves, too. Add 2 tablespoons of apple

cider vinegar. You won't be able to taste it in the finished product, but it helps pull out the nutrients.

3.  Fill the crockpot up completely with water. Put the lid on, set it on low, and leave it for 24 to 48 hours.

4.  Allow it to cool, then strain the liquid into jars or Ziploc bags. You can pressure can it, freeze it, or leave it in the refrigerator for up to 5 days.

You can sip it from a mug or use it as a base for other soups. This is a wonderfully healthy habit to get into.

### 10 Tasty Ways to Magic Up Your Mac & Cheese

Those ubiquitous boxes of macaroni and cheese powder never fail to remind me of one of the most broke points in my life when the 33-cent (at the time) boxes were all we had standing between us and real hunger. Now, boxed mac and cheese isn't the healthiest food in the world, but there are quite a few ways you can jazz it up, use it to extend leftovers that aren't enough to feed the whole family, or feed a large group of kids.

**1. Go organic.** If you're concerned about the icky ingredients in the cheap store brand, watch for sales on the organic brands like Annie's and Horizon. I've gotten them recently for as low as $1 per box. If your family avoids wheat, there are also gluten-free options.

**2. Serve it as a side dish.** My kids to this day love a side dish of boxed mac and cheese. Personally, I prefer the homemade baked kind with a crunchy topping, but if they're willing to go cheap-o, sometimes it's nice to have that choice.

**3. Hack homemade mac and cheese.** Speaking of the homemade kind, that stuff is pricey with all the real cheddar, cream, and butter you need. But, you can hack it inexpensively using a boxed kit as the base. Prepare the macaroni and cheese according to the instructions on the box. Butter a baking dish and spread the prepared mac and cheese into it. Stir in ½ cup of cream cheese. Top it with a good quality shredded sharp cheddar and some bread crumbs, crushed potato chips, or cracker crumbs. Bake it at 350°F, uncovered, for 25 minutes. You'll love the gooey goodness that tastes really close to homemade at a fraction of the price.

**4. Use condiments**. My kids grew up in Canada where everyone puts ketchup on their mac and cheese. Don't knock it 'til you've tried it! I like to jazz mine up with barbecue sauce or hot sauce.

**5. Turn it into a more flavorful side dish.** Have you ever used those "Sidekick" packages of pasta? My daughter recently recreated one of her childhood favorites using white cheddar mac and cheese, garlic powder, onion powder, and parsley flakes.

**6. Turn it into primavera.** Throw in a bag of frozen mixed vegetables of your choice while the pasta is cooking. My family likes the California mix with broccoli, cauliflower, and carrots. I'm allergic to broccoli but love it with cauliflower and lots of black pepper.

**7. Stir in a fancy cheese.** Use just a little bit of a more expensive cheese to add a whole new flavor. We've tried this with smoked gouda, extra sharp cheddar, sun-dried tomato Havarti, fresh Parmesan, and garlic goat cheese. Remember, a little goes a long way!

**8. Make it Mexican.** Do you have leftover taco meat or leftover chili but not enough to feed the whole fam? Stir it into prepared mac and cheese and heat it all together until it's hot and bubbly. This is sort of reminiscent of Hamburger Helper, but yummier.

**9. Make your mac and cheese blush.** Add some marinara sauce to prepared mac and cheese for a nice blush sauce. If you have leftover spaghetti sauce with meat, it's like an Italian version of Hamburger Helper.

**10. Hide some veggies.** If you're trying to hide vegetables to get your kids to eat them without complaint, cook and puree carrots or cauliflower and mix them into the sauce. They're hardly noticeable.

## Leftover Magic

In these times of tight money and ever-increasing expenses, we can't afford to let anything go to waste. One way to stretch your food budget is with the humble leftover. Have you ever been really poor? I don't mean "I can't afford Starbucks until my next paycheck" poor. I mean "Should I buy food or pay the electric bill before the power gets shut off" poor. I have absolutely been that poor, back when my oldest daughter was a baby. When you are that broke, every single bite of food in the house counts. You cannot afford to let anything go to waste. This is where the "Ménage à Leftover" bucket in the freezer comes in.

## Ménage à Leftover

In our freezer, we kept an ice cream tub. After each meal, those tiny amounts of food that don't add up to a full serving got popped into the bucket. And because of our situation, I often would take food that was uneaten on a family member's plate to add into the bucket. Desperate times, desperate measures. What people might consider "gross" in good times, they would feel lucky to have in bad times. Then, usually about once per week, the contents of that bucket in the freezer were turned into a meal.

I drew some criticism from friends and relatives during that time for the distance I went not to waste a single bite of food. A few people commented that it was ridiculous, others thought combining all those different foods in the freezer was "disgusting," and one person even referred to the meals as "garbage disposal meals." It stung a little at the time, but looking back, I'm glad to have had that experience. I can draw upon it if times become difficult in the future. While other people are trying to figure out where their next meal is coming from, I know that I can take the same amount of groceries and make at least two more meals out of them.

I always considered meals from the leftover bucket to be "free food" because they were items that you'd normally throw out. So, let's say you have a little bit of broccoli, some mashed potatoes, some beef gravy, a scoop of ground beef, some corn . . . you know? The remains of meals. What can you do with that? This is where being creative with the spices comes in. I might take the above, add a can of beans and a tin of tomato paste, and turn it into a chili-flavored soup. Alternatively, I could stir in some yogurt and some noodles and make it into a creamy casserole, well-seasoned with thyme. I could sprinkle a bit of cheese on it, wrap it in pie crust, and make turnovers. The trick is to make something totally new and different from it so that it doesn't even seem like leftovers. Some of the concoctions were absolutely delicious— so good that we recreated them with fresh ingredients later on. Others were not-so-great. Only a couple of times did we end up with something that was really so awful we couldn't manage to eat it.

If you can serve your family one "freebie" meal per week that results in a savings, for a family of 4, that equals about $100 to $520 over the course of a year. It doesn't sound like much until you add it up, does it? We don't always do the leftover bucket these days because times are not as tight as they were back then. However, we do creatively use our leftovers. Here are a few ways to remake leftovers into something new and delicious.

### Leftover Buffet

We have some nice little oven-safe dishes that are divided. We use these on "Leftover Buffet Night." Simply put, all the items from the fridge are placed on the counter. Everyone takes their divided dish and helps themselves to whatever leftovers they'd like for dinner. The dish is then placed in the oven and heated up—sort of like a "TV Dinner" of choice. If you use a microwave, you can just dish things out onto a microwave-safe plate and nuke each meal individually. Aside from the kids scrapping it out over the last enchilada, this is generally very successful.

### Leftover Soup

When I don't have quite enough to make two full servings, but it's a bit more than one serving, I often make soup. I can broth on a regular basis, so it's an easy thing to grab a jar of broth, chop up the meat, and add some vegetables and a grain. You can stretch your soup by adding barley, pasta or rice. If you have fresh bread to serve with it and a little sprinkle of Parmesan or cheddar for the top, you have a hot, comforting meal for pennies.

### Cream of Leftover Soup

I use this technique quite often with leftover root veggies. Using a food processor, puree potatoes, carrots, turnips, parsnips, or other root vegetables. You can add milk, broth, or even water to thin the puree to the consistency of soup. Season with garlic powder, onion powder, and other appropriate spices, and garnish with a tiny amount of bacon, chives, cheese, or sour cream. Other vegetables that are suited for puree are cauliflower, broccoli, and squash.

### Leftover Pie

This is a great way to use up leftover meat and gravy. In the bottom of a pie pan or cast-iron skillet, stir meat that has been cut into bite-sized pieces with gravy. If you don't have leftover gravy, a creamy soup, béchamel sauce, or thickened broth will work. Add in complementary vegetables, also in bite-sized pieces. We like peas, corn, and carrots with poultry, and green beans, carrots, and potatoes with beef. Add seasoning if needed. Top your pie with either a standard pie crust, corn bread batter, or with a biscuit dough topping. Bake as directed, then allow to cool for about 5 minutes before serving.

For even smaller amounts of leftovers (or picky eaters) you can use individual sized ovenproof containers or ramekins to make single serving "pies." I've also used muffin tins designed for the jumbo muffins to make individual pies. When using a muffin tin, you will want to make it a two-crust pie to enclose the filling.

## Leftover Hot Pockets

If I bake it in a pocket, my kids will eat it. Whether the filling is savory or sweet, there's something about a piping hot turnover that makes anything delicious. The key with a pocket is that the filling cannot be too runny. So, for a savory pocket, you can mix a small amount of gravy, tomato sauce, or cheese sauce with your meat and/or veggies, but you don't want it to ooze all over the place as soon as someone takes a bite. If you want to eat this as a handheld food, allow it to cool for at least 15 minutes before eating it.

You can use pie crust or pizza dough for your pockets. Pizza dough is our personal favorite because it is a bit more filling. I make pockets and keep them in the freezer. I take them out the night before and place them in the refrigerator. By noon the pocket is thawed and makes a delicious lunchbox treat at school.

We like pockets with veggies and cheese sauce; meat, mushrooms and gravy; meat and BBQ sauce; pizza toppings, marinara, and cheese; and meat and cheese. Another favorite is empanada style: meat flavored with Mexican spices, mixed with salsa, beans, and cheese. As well, you can fill pockets with chopped fruit that is topped with either cream cheese or syrup for a dessert-style turnover.

## Leftover Casseroles

The fact is, you can mix nearly anything with a creamy sauce and top it with a crispy topping and you have a tasty down-home casserole. (See the casserole formula on page 139 for details.) Try barley, quinoa, rice, pasta, or wheatberries to stretch your casserole. Instant comfort! For toppings, you can use stale bread that has been finely chopped in the food processor, cheese, crumbled crackers, crumbled cereal, or wheat germ, just to name a few items. I often use things that have perhaps become a bit stale—just another way to use up a food that would otherwise be discarded.

### Be creative!

You're only limited by your imagination when it comes to turning your leftovers into delicious, tasty new meals. Think about your family's favorite dishes. For us, it is anything in a pocket, pot pies, and creamy soups. So, when repurposing my leftovers, I try to frequently gear the meals toward those types of foods. A hint of familiarity makes the meal more easily accepted by those you are feeding.

## The Casserole Formula

I know, I know. Casseroles sound very "1950s Housewife." But when you're on a budget, casseroles are a great way to make a little bit of food stretch further in a tasty way. And, to make it even better, there's a formula. This is loosely based on Amy Dacyczyn's Universal Casserole recipe from *The Complete Tightwad Gazette*.

- 1 cup protein of choice
- 1–2 cups veggies of choice
- 1–2 cups carbs of choice
- 1½ cups sauce of choice
- Spices of choice
- Topping(s) of choice

It's honestly that easy. Your protein might be leftover meat, a can of tuna, ground meat, or beans. Your veggie can be any tasty thing you have that will go well with the meat. We often use either frozen or canned green peas, green beans, cauliflower, broccoli, or mixed vegetables. Your carbs can be pasta, rice, potatoes, or whatever grain you have kicking around in abundance. Your sauce is the "glue" that holds the whole thing together. It might be white sauce, gravy, a can of condensed cream-of-whatever soup, tomato sauce, or cheese sauce.

Casseroles are pretty yummy when they have some kind of tasty, crispy topping. This might be bread crumbs and butter, cracker crumbs and butter, shredded cheese, those little cans of French-fried onions—whatever tasty thing you have on hand. Season it with whatever spices you have that are appropriate—Italian seasonings, garlic salt, chili powder—whatever you think sounds good with your concoction.

To make your casserole, combine your cooked meat, your frozen or canned veggies, your cooked carbs, your spices, and your sauce. Bake at

350°F for 30 to 45 minutes, or until your sauce is bubbling. Then, add your topping and bake it for another 5 to 10 minutes until it is crispy.

## Have a Weekly Meal-Prep Extravaganza

When I worked outside the home, Sunday afternoon was always dedicated to weekly food prep. It was absolutely necessary to be able to juggle all of my responsibilities during the week ahead. Now that I work from home, I usually break food prep into two sessions, but the basic premise is the same.

**There are a lot of time-saving benefits to this.**
You only have one big kitchen clean-up. The rest of the week your dishes only consist of your plates and flatware, and what you used to heat your food in. You can multitask by having several things in the oven cooking at once—this also saves on your utility bill. You can also wash and prep all your produce at the same time, and then just wash your colander and cutting board when you're finished. Throughout the week meals are strictly grab-and-go. If your food is already prepped, dinner can be on the table in 10 to 15 minutes every night.

**What does a food prep afternoon typically consist of?**
- Menu planning
- Grocery shopping
- Washing and cutting up vegetables
- Washing fruit
- Portioning out snacks for lunch boxes
- Doing the baking
- Preparing some basic items that can be used in different ways throughout the week (chicken, beef, grains, salad)

When you prepare your food ahead of time, dinner is on the table faster than you can say "drive-through." Your budget will thank you because you won't require those impromptu pizza deliveries when you just don't feel like cooking. Your waistline will thank you because you won't grab high-calorie, low-nutrient convenience foods. Your health will thank you because you will be eating nutritious, wholesome foods from scratch that nourish rather than deplete.

I usually spend Sunday afternoons in the kitchen with my daughter. We turn on some good tunes, don some kitschy aprons, and get cooking. Here's a sample week of food prep.

- Yogurt parfait fixings
- 2 roasted chickens with carrots and potatoes
- Mexican-seasoned ground turkey
- Baked eggs
- Veggies for steaming
- Roasted Brussels sprouts
- Blueberry corn muffins
- Baked brown rice
- Garden salad
- Veggie packets for lunch boxes
- Bread

We also pack the barebones of our lunches for the week, too. Even though I work from home, it's nice to be able to just go to the fridge and grab what I want to eat for lunch.

**Here's a sample menu from my kitchen.**
For dinner this week, we'll recycle our prepped food into the following meals.

- **Sunday:** Chicken, carrots, potatoes, Brussels sprouts
- **Monday:** Turkey tacos with canned refried beans and rice, salad
- **Tuesday:** Creamy chicken and vegetable stew with homemade bread
- **Wednesday:** Leftover chicken stir-fried with prepped veggies and rice
- **Thursday**: Rice bowl with meat or beans, veggies, and salad dressing
- **Friday:** Homemade Mexican pizza topped with turkey, beans, and veggies; salad
- **Saturday:** A whatever is left free-for-all, fondly known as "Leftover Buffet"

Lunches and snacks are nearly always cobbled together from leftovers. Breakfast will be muffins, yogurt and fruit parfaits, baked eggs and toast, or smoothies.

## The Beauty of the Brown Bag

Brown bag lunches aren't just for kids! You can save a fortune each month by bagging up a lunch for the grown-ups in the family, too. And this includes those of us who work from home or stay home with the children, too.

Years ago, when packing two lunches for the girls each morning, I began to also pack a lunch for myself. I was in a workplace where lunch was a social event for many of my coworkers. Each day, they'd have a long discussion about where to go out to lunch. I went with them a few times but soon saw at least $50 per week drifting away with those fattening, unhealthy meals. That, of course, is $200 a month or $2,400 per year—a lot of money for a less-than-stellar meal, don't you think?

The same goes for school lunches for the kids. A school lunch averages $2.60 across the United States. Which works out to $13 per week, $52 per month, and $468 over the course of a school year. *Per child*. If you have more kids, you'll need to multiply that number again. So, a quick calculation: In a family with two adults working outside the home and two children in school, if all of those meals are purchased, you could be looking at a whopping $5,736 per year *just for lunches*.

Think about what you could do with that extra money each year if you worked lunches into the weekly grocery budget. It could be a vacation, a huge chunk of money paid off of your car loan or mortgage, or a nice cushion in your emergency fund.

**And then there's health.**

Cheapskatery isn't the only reason to brown bag it. The food we purchase away from home is rarely as healthful as what we'd eat if we bought it and prepared it ourselves. Restaurants take shortcuts, spray their produce to keep it looking bright, and often use the least expensive ingredients possible (read: artificial or loaded with pesticides.) School lunchrooms aren't noted for their fantastic nutrition either, and they're subsidized with the lowest priced goods the USDA can get their hands on. When you prepare your lunch at home, you can be careful to avoid allergens, buy organic, and select whole foods instead of processed ones. And really, when you think about it, good health can save you a lot of money too.

**Easy tips for brown-bagging it.**

Here are some tips for people who say that they don't have the time to brown bag.

- **Make lunches when you are cleaning up the kitchen after dinner.** Add leftovers to containers that can be heated up at the office. Put aside a serving to heat in the morning and add to a thermos for the kiddos. Put sliced fruit and veggies into Ziploc bags for snacks. My kids always preferred to assemble their own sandwiches at school, so for them, I'd place leftover meat in a Ziploc bag and a bun in another bag.
- **Prep some of your lunches during your weekly meal prep extravaganza.** For future lunches, you can portion out treats like cookies, sliced veggies, dip, and salads to grab when you're in a rush. If you sort this all out on your meal prep day, grabbing lunches will be a snap.
- **Teach the kids to make their own lunches.** I saw a cute system on Pinterest that brought back memories. You can grab some inexpensive plastic tubs to set up in the fridge with numbers on them. The numbers are for how many of the items in that tub your child can take in their lunch box. So, for example, 1 protein, 2 veggies, 1 fruit, and 1 treat. Stock it on Sunday night, and the kids will be all set to quickly grab lunches each morning.

**Get some cool containers.**

Lunches are a lot more fun if you have nice containers, and this goes for grown-ups too. Think about adding the following reusables which will save you money over the course of the year:

- Insulated lunch bags
- Glass containers (for adults)
- BPA-free Tupperware containers (I still wouldn't heat these up)
- Reusable sandwich and snack bags
- Thermoses
- Bento boxes (they are really cool looking)

# BYOBeverages

Of course, don't forget how much money you can save by bringing your own beverages, too. Every bottle of water you purchase is going to run you at least $1 (and sometimes $2). Each drive-through coffee you grab is going to be anywhere from $2 to $6, depending how fancy you get. Even if you end up bringing a can of soda pop with you, it's going to be a fraction of the price if you bring it from home.

Here are a couple of ideas.

- **Reusable water bottles:** Get one that is dishwasher safe and run it each night with the dinner dishes. Refill it with filtered water from home and store it in the fridge until time to go.
- **Thermoses:** I used to take a big thermos full of coffee, doctored up exactly how I liked it. Then I could indulge all day long at work.
- **Pre-packaged drinks:** Soda pops, juice boxes, bottles of iced tea—they're all cheaper purchased in bulk when you go grocery shopping. And if you know you're just going to grab it from the vending machine, you might as well bring it from home, right?

If you add the cost of beverages to all of the other "getting food out" expenses, you've easily added another thousand bucks to your budget over the course of the year.

# Part Seven
## Shopping Frugalite-Style

### Once-a-Month Shopping and How It Saves You Money

What would happen if you only went shopping once a month? Would you become more organized? Would you become more creative? Would you become more mindful of waste? Would you save a ton of money? Try this once a month shopping challenge. It's time to get down to business—the business of cutting your future grocery bills in *half*.

*The "Rules"*
You can change these around to fit your family's needs, of course, but here are our family's guidelines to the once-a-month shopping challenge.

**We are allowed one trip for each of our needs: groceries, animal supplies, and other supplies.** These may all be undertaken on the same day, or they can be split up based on the way your family gets paid.

**We spend some time checking out the sales at various stores in our area.** We make a day of it, hitting several different grocery stores after checking the sale flyers online.

**Supplies that can be obtained outside of regular retail environments are exempt.** For example, if you barter with a neighbor, purchase some craft supplies at a yard sale, or get a bushel of apples directly from a local farmer, these things don't count as "going to the store." This is a way you can make up for a shortfall in your supplies while still abiding by the "no stores" rule. However, ordering a new item from Amazon or another online retailer would be considered cheating.

**We allow two meals out per month.** This might be Chinese takeout, pizza delivery, or a restaurant meal. A meal out can break up the monotony and help you stick to your no-stores challenge. Based on your budget and your family's habits, decide if and how many meals you'll have out.

**Don't hesitate to break the rules if it's a matter of health or safety.** Obviously, I don't want to see your dog starve for a week because you underestimated the amount of dog food that you required for the month. Nor would I want someone to go without safety goggles at a new job until the end of the month. Adhere to the no-stores rule only if it makes sense.

If you have health reasons that require you to eat more fresh food, then by all means, work in a second shopping trip each month to pick up those items. My daughter who is dieting will require some extra veggies to munch on and we'll be making another trip two weeks into the month to supply those needs. Always use common sense with these challenges.

**Here's how to get started.**
Plan a trip to each type of store that you use. If money is a problem, you can split these shopping trips up.

- A trip to the grocery store
- A trip to a general merchandise store like Target or Walmart
- A trip to the feed store/pet store if it's necessary for your family

With each trip, you're going to predict what you need to run your household for an entire month. The next section will go into more detail about these shopping trips.

**Here are the financial benefits.**
As prices go up, it's easy to spend a little here and spend a little there until you are shocked to discover that you have nothing left. The easiest way to prevent that might be to stay away from temptation. Doing your shopping only once a month will help you stay away from those impulse purchases that always

seem to hop into the cart. It will be easier to keep track of your spending if it's all in one large trip.

After we moved, we got into the habit of "just stopping to get one thing" several times per week. This added up, and our grocery bill got out of control. When you set yourself a monthly budget, it can be difficult to keep track if you run to the store all the time. But when you shop once a month, you can withdraw the cash you need to purchase your items and stay within your budget more easily. This will also encourage you to dip into your stockpiles for those additional items that you might need to get through the month.

When I did this before, it made a massive difference in my grocery budget, and I think you'll see the same results. After the first month, it's far easier to shop this way because the money will be readily available when you haven't shopped for several weeks.

### Here are the organizational benefits.

If you know you only have one shot at getting all your supplies for the month, you're going to be far more organized about that shopping trip. You'll be forced to calculate your needs in advance so that you can get everything you'll require. You'll need to consider things like special events that are coming up during the month (are you celebrating any birthdays or holidays?), guests that may be arriving, and outings for the kids that might require snacks or certain supplies.

During the month, you can keep a list as you discover things you'd normally "run to the store" to pick up. This list can be fulfilled during the next monthly shopping trip, at which time you may discover you that you already found a satisfactory substitute for the missing product.

### Here are the creative benefits.

When you shop on a monthly basis you'll find that there are many ways to skin a theoretical cat. (Don't skin a real cat. I like cats. A lot.) If you run out of an item during the month, it's time to put on your problem-solving hat and come up with a replacement that doesn't come from the store. Maybe you can repurpose something you already have. Maybe you can create the item out of supplies you have on hand. Maybe you can find it at a yard sale, borrow it from a friend, barter for it, or simply live without it. Whatever way you find around the missing item, it's sure to get your wheels turning.

## Tips to Successfully Incorporate Once-a-Month Shopping into Your Life

Okay, so you're going to dive into once-a-month shopping, but how do you get started? I did this challenge myself a few years ago, and the following tips are things I learned in the process. In fact, I saved so much money that I really want to get back to this way of shopping.

- **Make a menu plan before you go shopping.** Even if you veer from the plan, you'll still have the ingredients on hand to make full meals. I like to plan out five dinners per week and leave the other two (plus lunches) open for leftovers. I can cheerfully eat the same thing for breakfast every day, so that's very easy to calculate.
- **When planning, think about what the ingredients are.** Plan to have meals with the freshest ingredients first, then the longer lasting ingredients, then the shelf-stable or freezer ingredients. Examples below.
- **Week 1:** Foods that are quick to spoil, like salad greens, asparagus, green beans, broccoli, peppers, fresh berries, bananas, zucchini
- **Week 2:** Heartier produce like carrots, Brussels sprouts, pears, oranges, cabbage, leeks
- **Weeks 3 & 4:** Now's the time to switch to frozen fruits and vegetables. (You can also use canned or dehydrated. We absolutely love applesauce, for example, and that works well as our week-four fruit.) Some things that will last well into the fourth week if properly stored are carrots, potatoes, winter squash, turnips, rutabagas, apples, and sweet potatoes.
- **Head to the store.** With these guidelines in mind, when you go to the grocery store, pick up enough fresh fruits and veggies to get you through a couple of weeks. Then, be sure that you have enough frozen, canned, or dehydrated products to see you through the last two weeks.
- **Pick up enough dairy products for the month.** If you have the space, you can easily freeze milk to be used later. The higher the percentage of milk fat, the more you may need to shake it up after it thaws. Cheese freezes well, but you should expect it to crumble instead of slicing when it thaws.
- **Sour cream tips.** It can be frozen if you are planning to use it in baking or cooking but isn't very good if you intend to use it as a

condiment. Instead of sour cream, try homemade plain yogurt. It tastes very similar and is quite simple to make yourself. (You can learn how to make yogurt on page 120.)

- **Eggs will be fine for an entire month in the refrigerator.** Think about how many eggs your family eats and stock up. If you don't have enough refrigerator space, you can freeze one egg per square in an ice cube tray, then move them into a freezer bag when they've frozen solid.
- **Keep your storage spaces in mind when you're on your shopping trip.** You want to be careful not to get more frozen goods than you can cram into your freezer and fridge. Opt for shelf-stable options if you don't have enough fridge and freezer space.
- **Think about fresh greens.** Start working on those solutions for fresh greens when you can't go to the store: sprouting, a windowsill garden, a greenhouse, a hoop house.
- **Think ahead about your month.** Do you have any special occasions to prepare for? Any birthdays or school parties or potlucks or guests? You'll want to have the right supplies on hand for any unusual events.
- **It's not just about food.** Next, move on to things like toilet paper, laundry soap, dishwasher detergent, and bleach for the month. Keep supplies on hand to make your own if you run out. (Better yet, start off with the supplies and make your own to save money!)
- **Remember health and beauty aids.** Don't forget about personal hygiene items like toothpaste, toothbrushes, shampoo, deodorant, and female supplies. Better to get a bit too much than not enough!
- **Get supplies for furry, finned, and feathered friends.** How much do your pets and livestock need to get through the month in good health? Pick that up at the store and stash it away.
- **Grab OTC meds.** Do you have things like over-the-counter medications and special foods in case someone is under the weather? It's best to stock up on these things ahead of time instead of waiting until you need them. Trust me, as a single mom, when I'm the one who is sick, it's horrible to have to go to the store to pick up medication or ginger ale.

You'll probably have some hiccups the first time you do this, but it will save you all sorts of money in the long run.

## What to Buy at the Dollar Store (And What You Should Splurge On)

There's little that gives me more of a rush than going into the dollar store and finding things for only a dollar that I would normally buy elsewhere. And they have a lot of other stuff that I've never seen that seems like a great deal. But the question is this: what at the dollar store is actually a good deal and what should we spend a little bit more on?

**What to buy at the dollar store.**

These are items you can get at the dollar store without any significant health risks (of which we know, anyway) and that aren't so flimsy that they'll break the first time you use them.

- Balloons
- Band-Aids
- Bobby pins
- Brooms and dustpans
- Buckets
- Coffee filters
- Coloring books
- Cotton swabs
- Dish towels
- Envelopes
- Fabric shopping bags
- Feather dusters
- Gift bags and tissue paper
- Gift wrap
- Greeting cards
- Hair elastics
- Index cards
- Name-brand food (check the expiration date carefully)
- Napkins
- Notebooks
- Paper cups
- Paper plates
- Party décor
- Pens and pencils
- Picture frames

- Poster board for those school projects and yard sale signs
- Pregnancy tests
- Puzzles
- Reading glasses
- School supplies
- Seasonal décor
- Socks
- Spray bottles for homemade cleaning supplies
- Storage containers
- Tape
- Toothbrushes
- Vases
- Washcloths

**What *not* to buy at the dollar store.**

At the same time, there are other things I would *not* buy at the dollar store. A lot of the items there are imported from countries with different safety standards than ours, so my rule of thumb is that I won't buy food or things that come into contact with my food, unless it is a name brand that I recognize and would buy at the grocery store.

For example, our local dollar store had some Betty Crocker brand whisks and cooking utensils and I was okay with that. I wouldn't have bought a no-name one there, however. Part of this is my concern about lead, cadmium, and arsenic. If this is a worry for you, check out the YouTube channel Creative Green Living. These ladies run around stores with a handheld device, testing things for toxic metals until they get kicked out.

- Anything you put on your skin
- Baby bottles
- Baby wipes
- Batteries (they may leak)
- Children's dress-up cosmetics
- Dishes
- Electronics (total junk that will stop working fast)
- Extension cords
- Glassware
- Jewelry (often contains lead)
- Knives (dull knives are dangerous to use)

- Off-brand food
- Pet food
- Plastic cooking utensils
- Tools (dangerously flimsy)
- Toys
- Vitamins

Of course, there are never hard-and-fast rules. If it is a product you normally use, do your due diligence. If it smells okay, looks okay, and is well within the best-by or expiration date, you may have found yourself a great bargain!

## The Ultimate Guide to Yard Sale Shopping

My favorite thing about the warm sunny days coming up isn't going to the beach or getting a nice tan. It's yard sale season! You can get a lot of stuff at a great price if you don't mind getting up early on the weekend and making the rounds of yard sales in your area. But, at the same time, you can also blow a lot of money on things you don't need.

Just like everything else, the key is to have a plan.

### What do you actually need?

The key to savvy yard saling is knowing what you need/want. Every year, I write out a wish list that I keep in my wallet. This year's list includes:

- Books (I'm always on the lookout for something to read)
- A decorative table that goes over the litter box, so I can disguise it
- T-shirts
- Mason jars
- Camping gear
- Food storage supplies
- Pet accessories
- Cabinet for sewing supplies
- Instant Pot
- Wooden salad bowl
- Solar gadgets

The list includes measurements of all types. I know what size that decorative table needs to be. I've measured the empty spaces that could house an item of furniture, so I don't end up with something too big. I know what size everyone in the family wears in clothing and footwear. This doesn't mean that I can't buy other things I see, but it helps keep me on track. Also, having the measurements at hand is convenient when trash-picking on the side of the road (much to my daughters' dismay).

## What is your budget?

The next step to yard sale success is sticking to your budget. Even when you're buying things at yard sale prices, you still run the risk of overspending. For this reason, I take cash in small denominations and only the amount that I intend to spend. For my daughters, when they were younger, I would provide them with a small amount of their own money to spend at the sales. This helped them to develop some control over finances even when they were little. It also kept them from constantly begging me for things.

So, for example, next weekend, I might take $50 with me in 1s and 5s. This allows me to negotiate with someone without pulling out a $50 bill. Occasionally, when you come across something way too good to be true, you may end up making a run to the bank machine to grab more cash. Be very careful when you do this—you don't want to affect the rest of your budget for the splurge. But if your washing machine is on its last legs and you come across a great one at a great price, you may want to grab it while you can.

## Methods of negotiating.

It is almost a given at yard sales that the sellers will be willing to negotiate. Here are the methods that I've found work the best:

- Ask prices as you go along, if the items aren't marked, and keep a tally in your head of what the total is.
- Pick up all the items that you intend to buy and discount it. For example, if they work out to $23, you might ask, "Would you take $20 for all this?" Because no one wants to carry all that stuff back inside their house, they'll often say yes.
- Don't be insulting. If something is marked for $200, don't offer them $50. It's not going to happen. If prices are already very reasonable, I generally pay the asking price, particularly if I'm only picking up one or two things.
- If they say no to your offer on a larger item, ask if you can leave your phone number. If they don't sell the item for the price they wanted, they may give you a call to take it off their hands at the end of the day.

**Before you buy something . . .**
When looking at items, ask these questions.

- Can I use it?
- Can I resell it for more money?
- Do I have room for it?
- Do I need it?
- Can I fix it?
- Can I clean it?

In the day and age of smartphones, it's pretty easy to look up an item online. If something is pricey, I check the reviews, I see what the new ones go for, and I check eBay and Craigslist to see if I can find used ones for sale for a comparison price.

**Planning your day.**
When I go "yard saling" it's an organized event.

- **First, I look through my local listings to see where all the sales are.** You can find yard sales advertised in your local newspaper, on Craigslist, and in local groups on social media. Write down the addresses and note what time they start and finish.
- **Map out the sales that you want to hit.** I do this in a way that is organized from furthest to nearest to my home.
- **Empty out your vehicle.** The night before we go on a yard sale spree, I empty out my vehicle of all but the essentials. I fold the back seats down to make more room, and I grab a handful of plastic bags to tote home my treasures. Be sure you have a full tank of gas, so you don't have to stop in the morning.
- **Get up early.** Be there a few minutes after an especially promising sale opens. Trust me, you probably won't be first.
- **Bring refreshments.** Refreshments are particularly important when you have kids with you. If you spend a ton of money buying coffee, soda pop, and fast food, you aren't really saving that much at the yard sales. I usually bring a thermos of coffee doctored up just how I like it, a cooler with water bottles, a sandwich, and some snacks.

Then get out there and enjoy your day!

# Part Eight
## Next-Gen Frugalities

Part of our role as parents is to teach our kids the things they need to know to go on and lead a successful life. We teach them to be kind, honest, and helpful. We spend hours per week driving them to and from extracurricular activities like sports and music. We teach them about morals and ethics. We give them skills like cooking, doing laundry, and driving. But one important skill that many parents omit is how to handle money.

## Teach Your Kids to Handle Money

When the kids grow up and get their first job, they have no idea how to create a budget, pay their bills, and have some fun. Many young people are buried in debt from student loans, the credit cards waved in front of their faces on college campuses, and the "easy payments" for everything from car loans to furniture.

The biggest gift you can give your kids is frugality. Maybe they won't ever be in a position in which they need to be thrifty, but statistically, more and more college graduates are ending up in jobs that are hardly enough to pay back their student loans.

### What if your kids refuse to get on board the Thrift Train?

All the frugal ideas in the world won't help if your kids (usually the culprits are teens) refuse to get on board your snazzy little Thrift Train. First of all, it's truly miserable to fight all day and all night with your teenagers. The scorn of a young adult is burning hot and icy cold at the same time. But in the end, you are the adult. You are the breadwinner. You are the one out there busting your fanny to feed and clothe His or Her Royal Highness. And as much as they may argue, wail, and rage, you are actually doing them a favor.

My advice is to press forward despite their youthful wrath. No, they aren't going to like it. Yes, they will inflict misery upon the entire house. But you also can't go into debt or go without food so that your middle schooler has the jeans he or she so fervently desires.

Here are three of the strategies that I used to teach my daughters to handle money while they were growing up. Interestingly, many relatives were utterly horrified that I was so open about money and money problems with them, but I sincerely believe that many valuable lessons were learned that will help them in their adult lives.

### Let them help pay the bills.

When your kids are old enough to feel entitled to things that may be out of your budget, it's time to pull out this important tool. Some people will strongly object to it, but I found that it did more to teach my kids about adult life and money than anything else I've ever done.

When one of my girls was about twelve years old, she wanted an expensive pair of shoes that "all" the other girls had. They were over $100 and totally out of reach for us at the time. I told her that we couldn't afford the shoes at this time. She had found my paystub and waved it at me. "Yes, we can! You make all this money!" I decided this was a teaching moment, so I opened my computer and pulled up my bank account. I grabbed all the bills we had to pay and then sat her down to teach her to pay bills online. She finished paying the bills and we still had a couple hundred dollars left. "See?" she said smugly. "We still have enough money!"

"What about food?" I asked. "What about gas for the car?"

We went to the grocery store and I let her help fulfill the shopping list. Then, we filled up the car with gas. When we got home, I opened the bank account again. We had about $70 left. She looked at the numbers solemnly and I could tell, completely understood why I wouldn't get her the $100 shoes. After that, I sat down with her once a month to do the bills and she grew up with a firm grasp on the reality of how much life actually costs.

### Get them to pitch in.

Another thing that I did with my girls was provide them with the opportunity to earn the things that they asked for. As most parents know, schools think nothing of asking for contributions of $30, $50, and even $100 or more for school outings. I always asked my daughters to contribute toward things like this, as well as birthday gifts for parties to which they were invited.

When they asked for the money, I would make a list of the age-appropriate chores they could do to earn it. If they didn't want to attend enough to do some work toward it, they could simply skip it. When they asked me why I wouldn't pay for these things like other parents did, I replied, "Why do you want *me* to work for your field trip when you aren't willing to work for it?" Throughout their teenage years, I kept a list on the fridge of things that could be done to get some extra cash. These chores are above and beyond the usual stuff of life, so they're things like painting the basement, washing the windows inside and out—you get the idea.

**It's important to teach kids about money.**

If you don't prepare your kids for the real costs of living, when they leave home, they will be totally blindsided. If you don't teach them the link between work and getting the things they want, they will always feel entitled. If you don't teach them how to stick to a budget, they won't know how to prioritize. While it sounds like tough love, teaching your children about money is one of the most important things you can do as a parent.

## Back to School on a Budget

Back-to-school time means there won't be any more daily cries of "I'm bo-o-ored!" It means the end of those impromptu trips to the beach or the pool. It means that your house will be a little tidier, you will get a little more done, and your kids will get to see friends that they haven't seen since the school doors closed at the beginning of the summer. Unfortunately, it also means that it's time for mom and dad to spend some money.

When many Americans can barely make ends meet from month to month without any additional expenses, back-to-school time can be the source of a great deal of stress. While we, as adults, can tighten the budget relentlessly on items for ourselves, many people have a much more difficult time enforcing frugality on their children. But by ignoring the financial restraints and spending with reckless abandon on our kids, I don't believe that we are doing them any favors. Showering your children with false prosperity doesn't prepare them for thriving in this world.

**Figure out your budget.**

First things first, a back-to-school budget is a must. This is dependent on your personal means. No matter what your child believes that they "need," it has to fit into the budget. For years, I have used the envelope method for things like Christmas and back-to-school shopping. It's fair, it's efficient, and it's tangible. This way, I not only stay within budget, but I teach my kids about budgeting also.

Both of my daughters are very financially responsible and handle money well because they have been making their purchases fit the existing budget since they were old enough to perform the necessary math to do so. There have been years that they made poor choices that they regretted, but because I allowed them to do this, they learned a lesson that you just can't teach them with a verbal warning.

1.  **Make two envelopes with each child's name on it.** One for supplies and one for clothes. Into the envelope goes a designated amount of cash—this may be $20, $100, or more, depending on your personal finances. (When making the back-to-school budget, be sure to keep your other expenses in mind—you still have to eat and pay your bills!)

2.  **Let them get some ideas.** Sit down with the kids and a pile of back-to-school fliers and tell them their budgets. Expect to hear lots of cheering and excitement as the large number floats around in their heads. Then hand them a notebook so they can write down what they need in two columns. Mark one column "supplies" and the other "clothes." Once they have written up their lists, have them go through the fliers and choose the things they want. Generally, their desires will greatly outstrip their budgets.

3.  *This is the critical teaching moment.* No, don't increase the budget! This is the time to teach them to figure out which of the items are necessary and which are optional. Have the kids consider their lists. Are there any items they have from last year that would allow them to strike some items off the wish list and free up some more funds? Do they actually *need* a new lunch box or binder, or will last year's suffice for just a little bit longer? If they get the $80 jeans, can they manage to purchase the rest of their wardrobe for only $20?

4.  **Spend a couple of days brainstorming.** Let your kids think about their budgets and their lists. You may be surprised at their solutions for stretching the money. They can search online for deals, they can get crafty and remake some of their own items—give them the freedom to be creative and to think for themselves.

5. **Go shopping**. Here are the rules. When you are in the checkout line, have your kids pay out of their envelopes. Receipts go back into the appropriate envelope, which makes it easier for them to see where their money has gone or to make returns or exchanges if necessary. If they are out of money they are finished shopping, unless they opt to take something back for a refund. This is the key element of teaching your kids to budget. *If you don't enforce this part of the exercise, you've completely wasted your time with the rest of it.*

My kids always had jobs in the summer—they babysat, did farm chores, and did one-time projects like cleaning out the garage, painting the fence, etc. While they were certainly allowed to supplement their budgets with their own money, quite often they saved for a bigger item or for spending money throughout the school year instead of spending their cash frivolously. Other times, they saved up for one big-ticket clothing item that they knew I wouldn't be buying for them.

**Budget-friendly tips.**
Here are some ways for kids to stretch their back-to-school dollars.

- **Clean your room.** You might find pens, pencils, and art supplies—then instead of buying new ones, you can allocate that money to other things.
- **Check out the business supply store.** Our local Staples has a great selection of 25-cent school supplies.
- **Check the fliers for loss leaders.** Walmart is selling loose-leaf paper two packs for $1. Just don't fall into the marketing trap of buying the overpriced items that are displayed by the loss leaders.
- **Visit thrift stores.** You can get nice things for a fraction of the price if you shop carefully. Plus no one else can copy your unique vintage style.
- **Go to the dollar store.** Items like pens, pencils, sharpeners, pencil cases, etc., can be found inexpensively there.
- **Focus on accessories.** Cool accessories can make last year's stuff look new.
- **Look at new ways to wear old clothes.** (This works better for girls than boys.) Last year's cool dress might be a cute top with leggings this year.

- **Refashion old clothes.** Turn outgrown jeans into a purse, or use pieces of old stuff to make headbands, scarves, or other accessories.
- **Do a dye makeover.** If you have some faded black items from the previous year, invest in a package of clothing dye, like RIT. They'll come out looking as good as new. You can also get other colors and dye things like jeans or T shirts. If you have an item with a stain that won't come out, dying it a darker color than the stain can give it a new life.
- **Wait until after school starts.** If you wait until after the first day of school, you may find that you require different items than expected. Shop for all but the most basic needs after you have gotten your list from the school. As well, many clothing items go on sale a few weeks after school starts, which will help your money to go further.

Back-to-school doesn't have to mean emptying your bank account or racking up your credit card bill. Shop responsibly and teach your kids the value of a budget.

## Why Susie's Mom Sucks

Does your child have a friend who seems to get everything he or she asks for? Are your child's friend's parents permissive to a fault? Are you constantly being compared to those other fine examples of parenthood? Let's call that friend "Susie." I'm here to tell you some harsh truths about Susie and her entire family. First, Susie's mom sucks. And secondly, Susie is probably a liar.

We've all heard it dozens of times.

"Susie's mom bought her $798 jeans."

"Susie's mom took the entire class to Disney World and everyone sat in First Class."

"Susie's mom lets her buy candy at the store every day."

Whatever.

First of all, is it even true? Or is Susie a lying little liar-faced liar? My guess is the second. There's always that one kid who wants to look more important than everyone else in the class. Or more innocently, they're totally mistaken about what's actually going on. Heck, when I was in first grade, I was convinced that my dad was actually the president of the United States and he just didn't want me to know.

And even if it *is* true, Susie's mom doesn't have your budget. Your bills. Your work hours. Susie's mom doesn't live your life. In all likelihood, if Susie's mom spends money like a drunken sailor, she is so deeply mired in debt that she'll never get out. Or she's actually Angelina Jolie and thus worth millions of dollars and can afford all that stuff.

You are not Susie's mom. You are your kid's mom and that means you make the rules about how money is spent in your house. You cannot be swayed by Susie and her mother.

**How do you tell your kid you aren't going to compete with Susie's mom?**

I'm not much of a coddler, so if you're looking for sweet answers, this could be the wrong book for you. The most powerful suggestion I have is to revisit the suggestions in the section about how to teach your kids to handle money, particularly the one about having them pay the bills. If that doesn't work, you may have a struggle on your hands. If a child is stubbornly resistant to reality, you may have to go with other strategies.

- **Talk to Susie's mom.** See if you can get to the bottom of the issue. She may not be aware of the way Susie is behaving.
- **Explain how bad other people have it.** Help them understand how fortunate they are to have a home to live in and clothes to wear and a bathroom instead of a place to squat outdoors.
- **Introduce them to some new friends.** If they spend all their time with families who have much different values and spending habits, it's going to be tough for them to grasp your own reality.
- **Take another look at what they're asking for.** Is there a workaround to provide them with it? Could you find the desired item on eBay or at a thrift store?
- **See if there's a way to help them earn it.** If you actually could afford the thing, find some age-appropriate chores that realistically show them the amount of work it takes to earn it.
- **Figure out why they're so adamant about whatever they're pitching a fit over.** If they're getting bullied at school because of their clothing or other things, you may have a totally different problem on your hands than simply "my kid is a greedy brat."

It's important to listen to your child and figure out why they want the things they want. You won't be able to teach them the value of frugality if they feel completely deprived.

## The Sleepover-Cheapover Survival Guide

Let me first say that sleepovers are a situation in which nobody actually sleeps. The kids are coming over to clean out your kitchen like a horde of locusts, scream loudly in unison, and break something. I hate to sound like a sleepover Grinch, but that's been my personal experience with sleepovers.

Here's how to reduce the expense of the little ~~horde~~ group of friends.

1. Fix snacks ahead of time. And fix approximately eight times as much as you think they'll actually eat. A group of twelve-year-old girls can mow through an astonishing amount of food.
2. Put generic chips in large bowls so that nobody knows they're generic.
3. Make lots and lots of popcorn. It's cheap and tasty.
4. Bake some homemade goodies like cookies and brownies. Resist the urge to add sedatives. Other parents will be mad.
5. Use 2-liter bottles of soda pop or water and smallish plastic cups with the kids' names on them. That will reduce the risk of kids opening cans and leaving them sitting around with only one sip taken out.
6. Kid-proof a room. You'll need a television, a music-playing device, and plenty of space for sleeping bags and dancing. Remove everything from this room that you would be heartbroken to lose. You can't imagine in your wildest ramblings the Machiavellian way that kids can break things.
7. Don't expect a lot of sleep. Groups of kids get really excited and that means they get really loud. If there are siblings in the house, see if they can visit a friend or relative for the night. Grab your own movie to watch and just let them enjoy themselves. In the grand scheme of things, one night of missed sleep won't kill you.

Sleepovers can be a great way to get to know the kids your child hangs out with. And they make priceless memories for your children to look back on. If you manage the food and potential of breakage, you can throw an awesome party without breaking the bank.

# Part Nine
# *Miscellaneous Thrifticles*

There are all sorts of ways you can save money on random things and ways you can reduce the temptation to spend with reckless abandon. These are some of my favorite random tips.

## How to Save Money with a Smartphone

Just about everyone has a smartphone these days and there are a lot of ways you can use it to save money. Of course, if you aren't a smartphone user, I'm not suggesting you run out and get one. You're probably saving more money than any of us!

Below are a few tricks I use to put my phone to work for me.

**The Target Circle App:** If you are a Target shopper, be sure to load the Circle app onto your phone. (This was formerly the Cartwheel app.) You can go through your shopping list before you hit the store and add "coupons" to an on-phone wallet to save big at the checkout. I often make my shopping list according to the coupons they have available. As well, you can also use your phone to scan items while you're at Target to see if there are any discounts available.

**Check for coupons:** I love hitting the craft store but it's *dangerous*. When I do go, I always check the online coupons to see if there are any that apply to what I'm purchasing. I've never gone to Jo-Ann's without saving at least 20 percent on yarn this way. (And who doesn't adore yarn?) Other stores like Michael's and Hobby Lobby have online coupons as well.

**Do your research before making a purchase.** Did you stumble across something that seems like a fantastic deal? Do some quick research before plunking down the money. Read the reviews (especially the brutally honest ones on Amazon) and see if there are any major consumer complaints. If something looks amazing on Amazon, be sure to run the URL through the website Fakespot.com. Fakespot analyzes consumer reviews to see if the stuff with positive ones are real or not. It's a lot easier to do your due diligence when all you have to do is grab a device out of your purse. Then, you can buy the item guilt-free.

**Compare prices.** Find out what the normal price is at other stores, and sometimes you'll find that the "deal" advertised isn't a deal at all.

**Get discounts.** Everyone's going mobile these days. My insurance company gives me a one-time discount for putting my insurance card on my device instead of sending me a printed copy. If you log in to the Wi-Fi at Kohl's, you get a discount on your purchase. You can keep a digital copy of any discount cards you'd normally carry, too, meaning there won't be any more issues of "Oh, it's in my other purse!"

**Download Grocery IQ:** This app is awesome. You can scan the barcodes of things you're running low on at home and the app will add the item to your list. But it gets even better. Grocery IQ keeps track of all your store discount cards and lets you know about deals, coupons, and discounts available locally on frequently purchased items.

**Use GasBuddy:** To make the most of this app, you will need to have your location services turned on. GasBuddy will show you the best prices for gas in your area.

**Keep track of due dates with BillTracker.** This app will send you reminders to let you know that certain bills are coming due. I have had the unpleasant experience of totally forgetting a water bill and going without running water for a weekend, even though I had plenty of money sitting there in my bank account. This app can help the forgetful among us keep more organized and avoid late fees. Plus, the calendar makes it really easy to budget your expenses.

**RetailMeNot saves you money in all sorts of establishments.** This app allows you to search for coupons for hundreds of stores. When you find the coupons you want, simply save them to your phone and they can scan it at the checkout.

**Go local with Groupon.** Groupon provides all sorts of deals on things like restaurant meals, services, and local establishments. LivingSocial is very similar to Groupon. These are deals offered by local merchants, gyms, and other providers. I generally like to call ahead to make sure I understand the terms of the discount.

**Get GoodRX.** This is a discount service you can use at pharmacies. Plug in the information about your prescription and GoodRX will show you which local pharmacy offers it for the best price. Then, you can have the coupon to guarantee that price sent to your phone as a text message. Use this coupon at checkout to save as much as 60 percent on prescription prices.

**Get great room rates with HotelTonight:** This app will help you find a room at unbelievably low prices at the last minute. In my family, we're big road trip fans. I've gotten some fantastic deals—I'm talking less than $20 a night at a nice hotel—by using this app the day of my stay.

## Walk the Walk: Frugal Fitness

Are you in the shape that you want to be in? If you're like me, expensive gym memberships and classes are out of the question. But that doesn't mean you have to skip fitness altogether. It all starts with a walk. Walking is the perfect exercise for nearly everyone and it doesn't cost a dime. Put on whatever shoes you have and go outside to let Mother Nature be your gym.

### Just walk.

Of course, there are many components to fitness, but the best place to start is to lace up your sneakers and walk. *(This is where I tell you, as I am legally bound to do, that you should seek the advice of your physician before starting this or any other exercise program.)*

When people start a walking program, they tend to make one of two mistakes.

1. They push themselves way too hard and end up getting so sore on the very first day that they are virtually crippled from Delayed

Onset Muscle Soreness. (Commonly known in fitness circles as DOMS.)

2. They don't push themselves hard enough and stop the second they begin to feel out of breath.

Your starting point depends on your current fitness level, of course, but that can be hard to judge if you have been moving from sitting on your rear at your desk at the office over to sit on your rear on the sofa at your house. So, I generally recommend that you start with thirty minutes. If you are truly sedentary, don't kill yourself by trying to set a rapid pace for your thirty-minute walk.

You should walk at a very comfortable pace for at least five minutes to warm up your body. Then, speed up to the point that speaking is possible but not super easy. Your heart rate should be elevated enough that your speech is limited to short bursts of words, not Shakespearean monologues. If you get to the point that you can only gasp out a word at a time, you are pushing yourself too hard, and you need to slow down. If you need to slow down, *that doesn't mean stop*. Keep going, just at a slower, easier pace. This is you, building your endurance.

Unless you are having the symptoms of an actual heart attack (extreme shortness of breath, faintness, dizziness, pain down one arm, etc.) keep moving at a slow pace as you catch your breath. About five minutes before your walk is over, drop back your pace a little to cool down. As you become more fit, you can make things more difficult. You can add hills, obstacles, increase your speed, carry a loaded backpack, or walk for longer to add to the challenge.

Here are some things that help motivation.

- **A dog.** My dog would walk *for-e-ver*! Walking a dog is a great way to keep motivated and will result in not only a healthier you, but a healthier and better-behaved pet too.
- **A buddy.** A walking buddy will help you maintain a pace. As well, we are much less likely to cancel our walk if a friend is going to be let down when we don't show up.
- **Tunes.** My playlist full of headbanging rock is my favorite piece of workout equipment. I opt for music with a beat that mimics the pace I want to keep. I like energetic, heavy-driving music to keep me motivated. Make a playlist of whatever inspires you to move quickly.

Sometimes I'll walk a little further just because there is a really great song on. I save this playlist for walks, making it a special treat.

*Safety note*: I recommend only using one headphone. Whether you are in the city or out in the woods, wearing two headphones and making yourself deaf is the equivalent of wearing a "Prey" T-shirt. It's important to always be aware of your surroundings.

**A word about excuses.**
Okay, a few words, because there are oh-so-many excuses.

**Don't worry about inclement weather.** Unless I am going to be struck by lightning or die of hypothermia because I've gotten soaked in sub-zero temperatures, I walk. There are many days that I look out the window at the gray skies and think, oh, man, I don't want to walk today! But I do it anyway. Why?

Because, you are training for *life*. You are training for events that happen at the most inopportune times. Rarely does a reason you need to walk conveniently time itself on a sunny day of moderate temperatures. Nope, if you have to hike away from a car accident, it likely happened because of ice or rain on the roads. You will be hiking away from it through the pouring rain.

If a crime has been perpetrated on you, and you must flee, are you going to take your chance when it presents itself? Or will you say, "Yeah, it's raining, dude. I'm just gonna hang out with this serial killer until it clears up."

You aren't made of sugar. You aren't going to melt. Just walk.

**And yes, you do have time.** Unless you are moving from the moment you get up in the morning until the moment you go to bed, you can find thirty minutes to go for a walk. Trust me, after you get used to it, your body will crave it and you'll feel so much better! If you really truly are that busy, break your walk up into two fifteen-minute walks, or even three ten-minute walks. There really are very few days that you can't take thirty minutes from your day to do something wonderful and potentially life-saving.

**You're sick?** Are you really, truly sick? If you are, you're right. You should stay home, tucked under the covers. But if you have a bit of a headache, low energy, menstrual cramps, or just general lethargy, you may be surprised at how much better you feel after a bit of exercise and fresh air. Exercise is nature's anti-depressant and sometimes those minor aches and pains are related to mood more than they are actual physical maladies.

You don't have to start with a Marine Corp Mud Run. You see all those big buff dudes running down the road in fatigues, carrying an 80 lb. pack? Let 'em run! You, my friend, are just going to walk today. You are going to get started and you are going to find your own path to fitness. This isn't about comparing yourself to those who are more fit or stronger than you. Everyone is not capable of doing what an Ironman Triathlete does but just about everyone is capable of more than they are doing right now. If you challenge yourself, you might just be amazed at what you can do once you've built a base of fitness.

**Get started.**

Today. Right now. If it's the middle of the night when you're reading this, then you can wait until tomorrow. But remember that the sooner you start, the sooner you will be fit. Getting into better shape is something you will never regret. Even if you never need to be more fit because of a survival situation, you still get all the health and well-being benefits from doing it. Your body and those who love you will thank you!

> "I got fit and never had to escape from a deranged stalker!
> What a waste of time!"
> —said no one, ever

Just lace up those shoes, get out there, and walk. Within a month, you will see that your thirty-minute walk takes you a lot further than it did when you began.

## Go Scorched Earth on Your Email

If your email is anything like mine, it's absolutely loaded with messages encouraging you to buy stuff. It tells you about new stuff that you just might like, things that vendors are positive you *need*, and the latest sales from your favorite stores. Honestly, your email can be a thousand times worse than the most persuasively displayed shopping mall when it comes to getting you to want to spend money because, often, you don't even need to leave your home to get the goods.

**My email was ripe for a good decluttering.**
A while back, I was scrolling through my messages, searching between all the advertisements for the personal messages from friends and family. I got sidetracked several times when I saw things that I wanted or that seemed like a great deal, and then I slammed on the mental brakes.

What on earth was I doing, inviting all this temptation into my inbox? There were messages from . . .

- The grocery store with daily sales
- Kohl's with their delightful fall clothing specials
- Wayfair, who is convinced I need a dining table after I made the mistake of clicking on one on Pinterest the other day
- The salon where I got my hair done once, offering me a coupon to come back and see them again
- Amazon, with about a half a dozen tempting offers for books from my favorite authors
- Domino's Pizza, who doesn't want me to have to cook dinner tonight
- FlyLady, who sincerely believes her cleaning products will make my life easier
- Martha Stewart, whose organizational tools could probably change my life

And that was enough to make me say, "I gotta go scorched earth on this email!" It was hard, though. I have gotten a lot of great coupons from a lot of my favorite stores via email. I have been notified of awesome grocery stock-up sales via email. I learn when books by my favorite authors come out, you guessed it, via email.

But the questions I had to ask myself were these:

- Am I saving more than I'm spending with all of these emails?
- Am I yearning for things I don't actually need with all these emails?
- Am I less satisfied with the things I have because of all these emails?

And the answer to all three questions was yes. *sad face*

**How to get rid of unwanted emails.**
The time had come. I had to go scorched earth for the sake of my budget and my happiness. There are a few ways to clean out your inbox. There are

tools like Unroll.me and Mailstrom that make it super easy to get rid of the unwanted clutter in your email. Do be aware that there are some privacy concerns with this, so if you use your email for anything sensitive you should do it manually instead. As well, remember the adage that if a service is free, *you* are the product. When these services snoop through your email, your data will be scraped and sold to the highest bidder. Some folks don't mind this, other folks do. It's totally up to you.

The other thing you can do is do it manually. This is what I did. When I sat down to watch some Netflix with the fam, I opened up my inbox (22,000+ messages, holy cow!) and I began unsubscribing from everyone who was trying to sell me stuff. It took me about an hour to get through it all, but it was time that I would have spent doing nothing productive, so I didn't mind.

**A quick note:** You can always find a link to unsubscribe near the bottom of your email. As someone who sends out emails on a regular basis for business purposes, I strongly urge you to do this instead of marking them as spam. Spam is for things you never signed up for or things from which you unsubscribed, but they refuse to get a hint. It really hurts businesses who send email to be marked as spam because it means that sometimes other folks who actually want the email must go digging through their spam folders to find it, and too many complaints can cause the service to refuse to work with you anymore. I know, this is personal, but I hope you'll consider what I'm saying here.

### Who gets to stay in your inbox?

There are a couple of places that send me truly good deals for things I need, so those folks got to stay. There were some places that sent extremely informative emails that linked me to interesting blog posts. Sure, they sell a few things here and there but the value I got from their emails was worth it.

When it comes time to do some shopping for some reason (maybe at Christmas and Black Friday and when my daughter goes job hunting and needs clothing) there are a few places I will re-subscribe to in order to get coupons. But as soon as my shopping is done, they're history yet again! So, set aside some time and get to unsubscribing!

## Beating the Rising Fuel Prices

If you haven't noticed the increasing prices of gas lately, you probably haven't fueled up. Across the nation, the prices are inching upward—in some places more than 30 cents overnight. New York City has reported the highest price I've seen of an astounding $5 per gallon.

Fuel is one of those things that we have to have, and we really can't stock up on in any significant way. While it's going to begin affecting the price of anything that must be transported (so, *everything*), this segment deals with personal fuel saving ideas.

**Fill up when it's cheapest.** Statistically, Monday is the day of the week when fuel prices are at their lowest, and Friday is when they are higher. The 4th of July and Black Friday are reportedly the cheapest days of the year to buy gasoline.

**Fill up in the morning.** Mornings are generally cooler, and that is when gasoline is denser. Later in the day, when it is hotter, gasoline expands. You will get a little bit more bang for your buck when purchasing fuel at the coolest part of the day.

**Figure out your area's cheapest gas stations.** But be warned, some places mix a bit of water with their fuel which can damage your engine. I tend to stick with places that are name brand to avoid this. There's an app called GasBuddy that can help you find the prices of your local fuel stations without driving around to them.

**Use the pump on low.** Instead of filling up the car as fast as you possibly can, take your time and use the low mode. This causes less vapor and you'll get your money's worth.

**Don't sit there and idle.** If you are stopped for any period of time, turn off your car. I know, it's hot.

**Know what uses up more fuel.** Putting your car in reverse, running your air conditioner, and accelerating use more fuel than driving at a steady pace. Your cruise control can help with this. Having your windows and sunroof open can increase drag, also increasing fuel usage.

**Maintain your vehicle well.** Keeping your tires properly inflated increases gas mileage by more than 3 percent. Doing a tune-up improves gas mileage by about 4 percent and repairing a faulty oxygen sensor can improve your mileage by as much as 40 percent.

**Use public transit.** This is why you have a car, to avoid public transit, right? But sometimes it just makes more sense to take the bus than to drive, pay for parking, then drive some more. If your teens want to go to the mall or movies, perhaps the city bus would be a better option than a parent driving them there, coming home, going to pick them up, and coming home. Weigh these factors into your transportation decisions.

**Group your activities.** If you have errands, figure out an efficient route. Group all the things you have to do on one end of town together instead of making multiple trips. Never go out for "just one thing."

**Hitch a ride and find some things to do.** For example, if your spouse works downtown, figure out a day of activities with the kids and hitch a ride. If someone you know is going to the city, ask if they'd like some company and walk to get some errands done or go sightseeing while they're tied up.

**Walk to things that are close by.** If you're anything like me, you have a habit of jumping in the car to go places that you could walk to fairly easily. If you live in a walkable area, transport yourself with your own two feet. Not only will it save on gas, it will help you get in better shape. If you have kids, the walk itself can serve as entertainment.

**Pack light when you travel.** If you are going on a road trip, keep in mind the fact that every hundred pounds of weight that you add to your car reduces the miles per gallon by 2 percent. That can really add up!

**Enroll in a gas station loyalty program.** I kinda hate those loyalty programs because I know that folks are mining my data from them, but they can save you a bundle on fuel. I have one from Kroger now and had one from Safeway when I lived in California. For every $100 you spend at the store each month, you get 10 cents per gallon off the price of gas at their stations. When you have lots of points, fill up when your fuel tank is nearly empty. Also important is to know when your points expire. Even if you have gas in the tank, use up those points before they disappear!

**Consider getting a more fuel-efficient vehicle.** This is only a good idea if you were buying another car anyway, but if you happen to be trading in, think about swapping your SUV, sportscar, or truck for a minivan or an economical car.

**Stay home.** Unless I'm actually traveling, I'm a homebody so it doesn't take much urging to get me to stay home. Days when I don't have to leave the house at all are the very best days, in fact. I know everyone does not share my deep affection for staying home. But, instead of driving around aimlessly or driving some place where you're bound to spend even more money, think about some ways to entertain yourself at home. Your wallet will thank you in many different ways.

# Part Ten

## Garden Goodies on a Dime

Just about every year, I plant a garden. No matter where I live, I find the room to grow something. Some years, it's super productive and I still have tomatoes in jars come May, and other years, it just helps with my bills in the summer. When your purpose for gardening is to decrease your food bills, your planning should be strategic, particularly if you have limited space. Here are some things to consider:

### What does your family love to eat?

For my family, it's tomatoes in all forms. In the summer, we slice them and enjoy with salt and pepper. In the winter, it's marinara sauce and chili. Because of this, I plant at least 10 tomato plants every year. Some breeds are specifically for sauces and soups, and others are for eating off the vine. Think about what your family eats again and again and plant accordingly.

### What can you buy super-cheap?

One thing I rarely plant is carrots. I can get a twenty-pound bag of organic carrots inexpensively at the grocery store. (They're sold for juicing so they're a little "uglier" than the fresh carrots you'll get in smaller quantities.) Another thing I can often get dirt cheap is potatoes. I wait for a sale on organic potatoes and then stock up, canning them, freezing them, and putting them in the cold cellar.

**What is really expensive at the store?**
Other things are much more expensive to buy, especially if you prefer organic, so those are the things to focus your limited time or space upon. A few examples are:

- Sweet potatoes
- Strawberries
- Heirloom tomatoes
- Sweet corn

**What can you grow prolifically?**
Some vegetable plants produce tons of food—more than you could possibly eat. For example, anyone who has ever had a zucchini plant knows that one plant will see you through a hungry summer and make you multiple loaves of zucchini bread well into winter.

Here's a list of some of the most productive veggies you can grow:

- Tomatoes
- Eggplants
- Summer squash (yellow and zucchini)
- Peppers
- Beans
- Okra
- Cucumbers

Even if you buy seedlings instead of starting them yourself, each of these plants will provide a lot of food.

**What will you make to see you through the winter?**
I already mentioned that I can marinara and chili, but it takes more than tomatoes to make those things. For example, I can grow nearly *all* the ingredients for these favorites:

- **Marinara garden:** Tomatoes, peppers, onions, garlic, oregano, basil
- **Chili garden:** Tomatoes, peppers, onions, chili peppers (I usually buy the pinto beans because it's cheaper for me than growing them)

- **Salsa garden:** Tomatoes, onions, bell peppers, jalapeño peppers, garlic, cilantro
- **Thai stir-fry garden:** Bok choy, onions, garlic, cilantro, purple Thai basil, green beans, broccoli

You get the idea!

**What grows well where you live?**

Every area has veggies that grow well and veggies that fail miserably. Think about the historical cuisine of your area and that will give you a good idea of the ingredients that will grow easily. For example, if you live in a hot climate, delicate greens are unlikely to thrive, but there are bolt-proof lettuces bred to withstand the blazing heat of Nevada that should produce well for you. But what if you don't have a place to dig in the dirt? Read on for tips that will help apartment dwellers be more self-reliant.

## Gardening When You Don't Have a Yard

Not everyone lives someplace with a big backyard or acreage. So, what can you do if you're an apartment dweller? Here are some tips to help you produce food, no matter where you live.

**Balcony/patio gardening:** If you have a balcony or small patio, load it up with veggies. These vegetables grow well in containers:

- Tomatoes
- Bell peppers
- Radishes
- Greens
- Bush beans
- Peas
- Zucchini

Note that you will need the proper support for plants that get tall or climb.

**Growing food indoors:** Maybe you don't have any outdoor space. There are several things you can grow indoors to cut your food bill.

- Fresh herbs
- Microgreens
- Spinach
- Sprouts
- Green onions
- Mushrooms (look for those sprouting logs)
- Ginger

If you really want to get into growing food indoors, you can invest in (or build) a hydroponics set-up, but those can be pricey.

**Look for a community garden:** Many cities now are turning abandoned lots into gardens for the community. You are assigned a little plot and can grow whatever you want in it. See the previous article for ways to make the most of your space.

**Go to the roof:** If your building has a rooftop, you may be able to persuade the other residents to turn it into a container garden space. Remember that rooftop gardens are very sunny and usually don't have any shade, so choose your plants accordingly. Be sure that there is a way to access water on the roof or you'll be lugging buckets up the stairs. No matter how good your intentions are, there will come a point in which you just stop watering your plants and they'll die.

Gardening without a yard isn't easy. It will require discipline and dedication. But if you really want to jump on board the backyard veggie train, you'll find a way!

## DIY Garden Supplements

If you set foot into any garden store at this time of year, you'll see loads of expensive soil amendments and supplements that seem like they're must-haves if you want to grow vegetables. They come at a high price at the store, but often, you can make them yourself at home using things that you'd normally throw into the trash. Here are some DIY garden supplements that will give you a flourishing garden on a dime.

- **Ashes:** Sprinkle ashes from your fireplace or woodstove onto the soil to increase potassium and calcium carbonate.

- **Banana peels:** If your soil needs potassium, plant banana peels in the dirt beside the roots of potassium-loving plants.
- **Coffee grounds:** Instead of dumping your coffee grounds, spread them out to dry. Then use them as mulch around plants that crave nitrogen, such as blueberries, avocados, and fruit trees.
- **Egg shells:** Rinse and dry out eggshells, then crumble them finely. Scatter them on your garden soil to add calcium and phosphorus.
- **Epsom salts:** Dissolve 1 tsp of non-scented Epsom salts into a gallon of water, then spray onto your garden to add a dose of magnesium and sulfur.
- **Hair:** Human or pet hair adds nitrogen to the soil. Bonus: It can also help repel deer and rabbits.
- **Tums:** I plant an extra-strength Tums pill at the root of all my tomato plants to help prevent blossom-end rot. You can also use powdered milk or eggshells for this purpose.
- **Urine:** I'm not even kidding. One part pee to nine parts water will provide a healthy dose of nitrogen to your soil. Tomato plants are particularly happy with pee-water.
- **Water from the aquarium:** The waste from the fish is a fantastic fertilizer for your garden.

Healthy soil is the most valuable thing you can add to a garden. To see what you need, either take a soil sample to your local extension office or get a soil testing kit. This will help you decide what supplements you need.

### How to make a quick $12 compost bin.

Have you ever priced out those compost bins that you can buy? They have all sorts of bells and whistles, like cranks that turn the contents for you and fancy slide-out trays at the bottom. They can also cost hundreds of dollars. Since that was totally out of my budget, I decided to make a simple DIY compost bin for a whole lot less money. Of course, you can always pile up a heap of compost in your yard or garden, and that's exactly what I did when I lived in the country. Now that I'm living in town, I decided I should be a little more civilized. Of course, not $300-for-a-container civilized.

Because we have raccoons, foxes, squirrels and other varmints, I needed a closed container, lest I lure the little $*%#s into my garden. So, I spent $12 to make a compost bin from a 32-gallon latch tote and it only took about 15 minutes. You can get these in all sorts of colors to blend with your fencing or outdoor décor.

This is the easiest DIY ever.

1.  Drill 6–12 holes in the bottom of your bin, then drill a few holes in each side. (The number of holes will depend on the shape of your bin
2.  Then, put the lid on the bin to provide a little bit of stability. Finally, drill another half dozen or so holes in the lid of the bin.

That. Is. It. Can you believe how stupid-easy that was? It's almost embarrassing how short this how-to is.

## Composting 101

Don't just go pile rotting produce in there or you'll have a stinky mess. You have to balance out the greens and the browns. (We'll talk about greens and browns in a moment.) To get your compost off to a good start, lay some ripped up cardboard or newspaper (not the kind with color, just black and white) in the bottom of the bin. Top that with some straw or leaves, then top that with some garden soil. You may need to buy a bag if you don't have any to spare. Fill your container about a third of the way with these items.

Place your bin in a convenient spot so that you don't have to climb a fence and hang upside down like a bat to get to it. Make things easy on yourself. I put mine right in the garden, lurking between a shrub and a small tree. This way, when my glorious compost-to-be is done, I don't have to lug it half a mile. I can just tip it over and spread it out.

### How to make the magic happen.

Now, let's create lush soil out of the stuff that people usually throw in the trash. The smaller the pieces are that you put into your compost pile, the faster you will have beautiful soil from it. You can run your fruit and veggie scraps through the blender and run outdoor clippings over with the lawnmower for best results. Paper can be run through the shredder.

Each time you add something to your compost pile, give a little stir. I keep a rake handle nearby for stirring things up. Things are decomposing when they're giving off a lot of heat. If there isn't any heat in there, your composting magic is not occurring.

Now, remember how I was talking about balancing your greens and your browns? Here's how that works. Things with lots of carbon are browns and things with lots of nitrogen are greens. According to CompostGuide .com:[1]

> The ideal ratio approaches 25 parts browns to 1-part greens. Judge the amounts roughly equal by weight. Too much carbon will cause the pile to break down too slowly, while too much nitrogen can cause odor. The carbon provides energy for the microbes, and the nitrogen provides protein.

To clarify: If your compost begins to smell bad, you need to add browns. If it isn't composting fast enough, you need to add greens.

**50+ things you can compost in your new DIY compost bin.**
Here are the browns and greens you can add to your compost pile, heap, bin, or whatever.

**Browns are things like:**
- Paper napkins
- Paper towels
- Toilet paper (not with human waste on it)
- Raked leaves
- Newspaper without colored ink
- Junk mail without colored ink
- Sawdust from untreated wood
- Pine needles (don't go crazy, they can be very acidic)
- Pine cones (also acidic)
- Straw
- Peat moss
- Shredded cardboard
- Envelopes (remove the little plastic window and shred the paper)
- Cotton balls (pulled apart)
- Shredded toilet paper or paper towel tubes
- Shredded egg cartons
- Crushed nut shells
- Shredded twigs and branches
- Coffee filters
- Lint from the dryer

---

1 "Compost Materials," Compost Guide, accessed on June 29, 2020, https://www .compostguide.com/compost-materials/

**Greens are things like:**
- Fruit skins
- Apple cores, but not the pits from stone fruits unless you grind them up
- Vegetable peels
- Vegetable trimmings (like the bottom of the celery)
- Fruits and veggies that have been in the freezer too long
- Grass clippings
- Clippings from shrubbery
- Potato peel
- Human hair
- Pet hair
- Egg shells
- Tea bags (remove the staples) and tea leaves
- Clippings from non-toxic houseplants
- Dead bugs
- Dead cut flowers
- Stale cereal
- Feathers
- Bread
- Leftover hot cereal
- Onion skins
- Leftover fruits
- Leftover vegetables
- Dust bunnies
- Banana peels
- Stale chips
- Stale crackers
- Coffee grounds
- Coffee filters
- Pet bedding from non-carnivorous animals
- Manure from non-carnivorous animals
- Contents of the dust pan
- Contents of the vacuum cleaner
- Pulp from the juicer

If the pH needs to be adjusted, you can add ashes from the fireplace or woodstove. Just a little, though, or you will turn your soil too alkaline and decomposition will not occur.

(Note: While the manures of humans and carnivorous animals *are* compostable under certain conditions, great care must be taken with that or serious food-borne illness could occur. Those instructions are not included in this article. Check out *The Humanure Handbook* if you want to take composting to that level.)

## Water-Saving Tips for Your Garden

Depending on where you live, your summer water bill may end up being sky-high if you are a gardener. Back when I lived in California, not only was our bill extremely expensive, but we were also limited to watering only twice per week. Because of this, I became an avid user of low-water tricks.

Here are some ideas to help you keep your water bill low this summer.

- Landscape with plants that grow naturally in your area. They should require little in the way of additional watering. Your county extension office is an excellent *free* resource and can often help with this.
- Take a hike and find many lovely plants that thrive whatever your climate happens to be.
- Grow organic. Chemical fertilizers can increase a plant's need for water.
- Use an organic mulch in your garden to help retain moisture.
- If you are container gardening, choose pots with water-saving features.
- When you clean out your fish tank, reserve the water for your garden. Your veggies will love the nutrient boost!
- Harvest rainwater for your garden. (In some places, where the government believes they own the water falling from the sky, subtlety may be in order.)
- Devise a gray water catchment system for your shower, your washing machine, and your kitchen. This water can be used for flushing, watering plants, and for cleaning. Do keep in mind that some counties do not allow gray water to be reused, even in the midst of an epic drought. Do what you will with this information.
- Use drip irrigation instead of a sprinkler to get water right to the roots of your plants.
- Use a nozzle on your hose so that you are only putting water where you want it, not spraying it uselessly as you walk to the garden.

- Water container plants in the early afternoon and bed plants in the morning for the most efficient usage of water.

Don't undo your grocery savings with high water bills. Conservation can save you money.

# Part Eleven
## Party Like a Frugalite

One thing I believe to be incredibly important when you set out on your frugal journey is not to deprive yourself of the simple joys of holidays. There's no faster way to make your family (and let's be honest, yourself) hate frugality than to take away treasured traditions. Family traditions and special moments are priceless but that doesn't mean they need to cost you the world. You can have holiday fun without breaking your budget. Here are a few tips to adapt for your own families.

### Dying Easter Eggs Naturally
Dying Easter eggs naturally may bring to mind outrageously expensive ingredients or fancy hipster egg-dying kits, but actually that couldn't be further from the reality of it. You can easily dye eggs using natural things you probably have in your kitchen already. The artistry starts with the eggs you choose. Brown eggs will be a bit darker and earthier, while white eggs will produce soft pastel colors.

Now, the fun part—coloring your eggs! Each process will take thirty minutes. For darker colors, boil your eggs in a solution.

- **Dark yellow:** Boil eggs with 3 tbsp turmeric, 1 tbsp white vinegar, and water
- **Burnt orange:** Boil eggs with yellow onion skins, 1 tbsp white vinegar, and water
- **Dark brown:** Boil eggs in black coffee with 1 tbsp white vinegar
- **Hot pink:** Boil eggs with 1 can beets and juice, 1 tbsp white vinegar, and water

- **Cobalt blue:** Boil eggs with 2 cups chopped purple cabbage, 1 tbsp white vinegar, and water

If they haven't reached the depth of color you want, let them sit in the hot water for an extra half hour. You can use the leftover water to make pastel-colored eggs.

For pastel colors, soak already boiled eggs in a solution that you've poured into a mason jar. To start off, make your dye, below. If you want only pastel eggs, don't cook any eggs in the dye solution. Just bring it to a boil, then reduce the heat and simmer the concoction for half an hour. Use a mesh colander to strain out the dying matter and pour your dye into a mason jar. Soak the eggs in room temperature dye for half an hour to an hour, until the desired color is attained.

- **Pastel yellow:** 3 tbsp turmeric, 1 tbsp white vinegar, and water
- **Peach:** Yellow onion-skins, 1 tbsp white vinegar, and water
- **Pastel pink:** 1 can beets and liquid, 1 tbsp white vinegar, and water
- **Pastel blue:** Soak eggs in room-temperature cabbage solution, 30 minutes
- **Mixed colors:** Soak in the first solution for half an hour and the second solution for 30 seconds
- **Purple:** Beet solution, then cabbage solution
- **Green:** Turmeric solution, then cabbage solution

## Using Up Your Easter Eggs before They Spoil

Now that you've made a kabillion Easter eggs with gorgeous natural dyes, what on earth will you do with them all? I hate wasting food, and Easter eggs are no exception. Here are some of the ways we use up our eggs so they don't spoil.

- **Deviled Easter eggs:** Serve them at your holiday dinner as deviled eggs. But, for a twist, put just a teeny bit of food coloring into the mayo/yolk mixture so that you have a tray of multi-colored deviled Easter eggs.
- **Egg salad sandwiches:** Egg salad sandwiches are a tasty way to use up extra eggs. My kids like egg salad made with honey mustard instead of plain yellow mustard.
- **Sliced egg on salad:** Make chef salads for lunches and slice hard-boiled eggs for the top.

- **Mix them into other salads:** We like chopped boiled egg in both tuna salad and potato salad. They're also tasty in a warm, German-style potato salad.
- **Pickled eggs:** In a saucepan mix together 1 can beets (with liquid), 1 cup water, 1 cup white vinegar, ½ cup sugar, and ½ teaspoon cinnamon (optional). Bring the mixture to a boil and stir until the sugar is dissolved. Remove the saucepan from heat, then pour the contents over the eggs. Place this in jar with a lid in the fridge overnight. (Do not soak the eggs in the brine in a metal bowl or they'll be gross and slimy.)
- **Scotch eggs:** Scotch eggs are boiled eggs that have been wrapped in bulk sausage meat, then rolled in bread crumbs, and then fried or baked. Google for delicious recipes so that you can use what you have on hand.
- **Egg au gratin:** Preheat the oven to broil. Cut 6 to 8 boiled eggs into 6 slices each. Layer the eggs in a well-greased casserole dish, slightly overlapping the slices. Sprinkle the eggs with salt and pepper to taste. Sprinkle shredded sharp cheddar cheese on the top of the eggs, then pour ⅓ cup of cream over the whole thing. Pop it under the broiler for 2 to 3 minutes, watching it carefully so you don't burn it. This is delish with toast for dipping into the creamy, cheesy sauce.

Although many people leave dyed eggs out all day on Easter, it's important to note that, officially, the CDC says that eggs should not be consumed if they are left out at room temperature for longer than 2 hours. They're safe to eat for up to a week if they're left in the fridge.

## Building a Bargain Easter Basket

On a budget but you still want to see your kiddo's eyes light up with delight on Easter? This section is not about building a healthful basket full of organic Easter treats. It assumes that you're okay with some less expensive chocolates and other candies.

*The "Basket"*

First of all, remember that the basket doesn't have to be a basket at all. Don't get lured into those flimsy dyed baskets at the discount store because they're not worth the money. Here are some frugal ideas for containing all the candy.

- **A secondhand basket:** If you want, you can spray paint it the color of your choice, but I've always been able to find very nice baskets at my local thrift stores.
- **Other containers:** I generally bought my girls containers that would be useful for organizing their rooms instead of baskets they'd never use. I chose their favorite colors and got them buckets, caddies, and plastic organizers in the past.
- **Gift bags:** Hit up the dollar store and look in the gift-wrapping section for gift bags in pretty Easter-y looking colors. You'll pay a buck, it'll look pretty, and the kids will be just as happy.
- **Something you have kicking around the house:** You may have appropriate gift bags lying around, unused baskets in the basement, or other interesting containers you can upcycle into Easter duty.

Make sure the containers aren't too big. If you get one that is absolutely huge, you'll be tempted to put far too much candy and other goodies in it.

### The "Grass"

You don't need to go buy bags of Easter grass at the store to fill up the bottom of your kiddos' baskets. Here are some other ideas.

- **Shred it at home:** Use colorful mail to make a rainbow of "grass" or use newspaper for a black and white effect. If you have old gift wrap that got too crumpled to use, that too could be shredded.
- **Use tissue paper:** I know that at many stores where I shop, they load up my bags with tissue paper. I always fold it neatly when I get home and put it aside for opportunities just like this one. I do the same with tissue paper that comes in any gifts we receive.
- **Use crumpled paper bags:** I know this sounds weird but, trust me, if you are going with a more natural-looking theme, take the brown paper bags from the grocery store, rip them into strips, and crumple them in the bottom of a rattan basket. It will look lovely filled up with chocolates. Brown paper bags can be shredded too, if you're married to that whole "grass" look.

If you decide you must have the colorful, store-bought Easter grass, hit up the dollar store and get it inexpensively.

*The "Goodies"*

Now, what will you put in your glorious basket? Here are some tips.

- **If there is some treat you always, always, always get, continue to get that.** (Unless it's outrageously expensive, in which case it's time for a new tradition.) Make this the centerpiece of the basket.
- **Get the candy in bulk.** Don't buy individual items. If you have several children, get several bags of candy and divvy them up among the kiddos.
- **Get some of those plastic eggs.** You can fill them with all sorts of small treats, like M&Ms, cream eggs, and jelly beans. My daughters absolutely loved opening them and finding those icky marshmallow chicks inside. And the eggs can be reused year after year.
- **Add some homemade treats.** One of my daughters was severely allergic to eggs, so every Easter I made rice crispy treats and formed them into the shape of eggs. I tied curling ribbon around them to make them look more festive.
- **Add some non-edible treats too.** Things like hair elastics, small puzzles, gel pens, water bottles, bubble liquid and wands, and other outdoor toys.
- **Add some stuff that could go in their lunch boxes.** I used to splurge on some treats that were individually packaged for my children's Easter baskets, like Goldfish, Teddy Grahams, and Fruit Roll-Ups. This way, they won't gorge on it the very first day and you'll have something fun to send to school the following week.
- **Think outside the box.** Lip balm, make-up, earbuds, razors, and shaving cream are great for older kids.

*Stuffed Animals*

Apparently, it just isn't Easter without a pastel-colored stuffed animal. I often picked these up at the thrift store, when they were cast aside barely used from previous Easters and Christmases. I also learned to purchase pink and purple stuffed toys right after Valentine's day that could cleverly be shoved into a basket with either the change of a ribbon or the removal of it entirely. Often, you can pick up some stuffies at the dollar store, if you absolutely must have something brand new. Honestly, with these kinds of things, my kids rarely played with them for long, anyway.

## A Dozen Thrifty Mother's Day Ideas

Despite what the TV commercials insist, most moms aren't yearning for diamond bracelets for Mother's Day, particularly if the budget is tight. Often, the best gifts cost nothing (or next to nothing). Below is a list of a few ideas when people say, "What do you want for Mother's Day?"

- **A day off:** How nice would it be if everyone pitched in to do laundry, cook meals, and clean up afterward for an entire day? This is my favorite gift ever.
- **Breakfast in bed:** This is a cliché for a reason—it's awesome! I love getting a stack of fluffy pancakes, a card, and a good book to read on Mother's Day.
- **Chore coupons:** Moms can exchange these coupons for your services on other days. Things like doing the dishes, cleaning the kitchen, mopping the floors, dusting, and running a load of laundry can be very welcome gifts on a day when Mom is frazzled and busy.
- **Love coupons:** My girls have given me coupons for things like hugs, kisses, painting my toenails, rubbing my neck, watching my choice of a movie—you get the idea.
- **Cleaning the car:** What an awesome surprise it is to go out to the car and discover that it has been vacuumed and wiped down!
- **Cleaning the house:** Send Mom out for the day and get that house spic and span before her return.
- **Kid-made dinner:** When the kids make it with love, even boxed mac and cheese is gourmet to moms.
- **Homemade cards:** I've kept all of the homemade cards my daughters have made for me over the years. They make me smile to this very day.
- **Go hiking or biking together:** We often go on a Mother's Day hike to one of our favorite places and bring a picnic lunch along.
- **Make a playlist:** Whether she uses iTunes, Spotify, or some other music service, create a playlist that you know she'll love. Add in favorite songs you remember her playing from your childhood.
- **Bake her favorite cookies or dessert:** Spend some time in the kitchen concocting her favorite treat.
- **Call or Skype:** If your mom lives far away, a call, or better yet, a Skype where you can see each other, will make her day.

I'll tell you the truth—what Moms want most is the gift of your time. That's it. You don't have to get fancy and spend a fortune.

## How to Have a Frugal 4th

Are you planning on having (or attending) some Fourth of July festivities? You don't have to break the bank to have lots of great food and activities.

*Decorations*

It's easy to put together some inexpensive Independence Day decorations. Hit up your local dollar store for the best prices.

- **Streamers:** There are few decorations that will give you as much bang for your buck as streamers will. Grab some red and blue streamers, and then you can twist them together as garland, tape them over a doorway like a ribbon door cover, and wrap them around bannisters and columns.
- **Balloons:** Red, white, and blue balloons can be blown up and taped into bunches. Tape them to straws to make festive centerpieces.
- **Little flags:** You can buy small American flags in bunches at the dollar store at this time of year. Pop them into planters, use them in centerpieces, and give them to the kids to wave.
- **Put out your flag.** If you have an American flag, this is the day to fly it!
- **Disposable napkins, plates, and tablecloths:** Pick these up in the dollar store too. If you go with a variety of solid colors instead of ones with designs printed on them, you'll get more bang for your buck.

Don't go crazy buying expensive decorations you'll only use once per year or throw away after the party.

*Food*

Of course, everyone loves delicious food, and this holiday is no exception.

- **Nothing says the Fourth of July like a barbecue.** This doesn't mean you have to serve steak and chicken breast, however. Opt for hamburgers and hot dogs for a more budget-friendly meal.

- **Make classic salads.** Instead of getting fancy, go with the classic side dishes like potato salad, coleslaw, and macaroni salad. These foods are easy to make and inexpensive.
- **Go potluck.** If people ask what they can bring, for heaven's sake, stop feeling like you have to do it all yourself. Ask them to bring side dishes and desserts.
- **Choose simple foods**. One of our favorite Fourth of July party foods is a simple mixed fruit bowl of strawberry slices and blueberries. It isn't fancy but there's never so much as a berry left over.

*Activities*

This is another place where it's easy to go overboard. Plan ahead so you have plenty of low-cost activities for kids and adults alike.

- **Ask everyone to bring their water guns.** Our Fourth of July would not be the same without our annual water gun battle. We stash big buckets of water all around the yard and ask friends to BYOWG (Bring Your Own Water Gun) for the battle royal. Everyone always gets soaked and has a great time.
- **Grab some water balloons.** While you're at the dollar store, don't forget to pick up some bags of water balloons. These can be filled up and used as extra "ammo" during the water gun battle.
- **Set up the kiddy pools.** If you have children attending, be sure to tell parents to bring swimsuits for them. Set up kiddy pools and any other outdoor water activities you may have.
- **Don't forget story time.** We always read the story of our nation's fight for independence before we kick off the festivities.
- **Get sparklers and glow jewelry.** One of the least expensive (and safest) fireworks is sparklers. Have fun with those at home, and pop on glow bracelets or necklaces from the dollar store too. (Any extra glow jewelry can be used during a power outage.)
- **Go to your local fireworks display.** Most communities have annual fireworks displays and it's usually free. This is a great way to finish off the night without spending hundreds of dollars on your own fireworks. Be sure to bring blankets, lawn chairs, snacks, and drinks.

Most of all, enjoy a summer day spent with the people you love.

## A Frightfully Frugal Halloween

You want to know what's *really* scary about Halloween? *The amount of money that people are spending on it!* In 2018, Americans spent—are you sitting down?—almost *ten billion dollars* on Halloween. And it isn't even a "gift giving" holiday like Christmas. More than two billion of those dollars were spent on the sweet stuff. The average spending for candy across the country was $16.45 per person. This included candy to eat themselves and candy to hand out. In Oregon, however, they hand out full-sized candy bars and the average in that state is $40.29 per person.

Home décor was equal to candy with 2.7 billion dollars spent. The average expenditure for spooky home décor was $37.70, according to one survey. Costumes clocked in at 3.4 billion dollars. Not only are we dressing up the kids, but we're also dressing up grown-ups and pets. Men spent an average of $96 on costumes and women spent $77. Which means a family of four is spending over $150 a year on Halloween decorations! Scary stuff. Families are spending upwards of $250 for *one night* of fun. This is the definition of insanity.

**You can still have fun without spending all that money!**
Here are some ways to be frightfully frugal but no less festive this Halloween. I would never say to totally ignore it because it's one of our very favorite holidays! Remember: epic Cheapskatery isn't about skipping all the fun. It's about doing it cheaper and without causing harm to your budget.

*Costumes*
- **Hit the thrift store.** You may find used costumes. If not, you will at least find the components for something completely unique.
- **DIY.** If you can sew, you can easily make your own costume. If you can't sew, look for ideas that use safety pins and fabric tape. I once made a truly glorious long pink tutu for my daughter with nary a stitch. We safety-pinned a waistband and pinned on a bunch of pink roses I found at the thrift store. She wore it with a black leotard and leggings she already owned. We topped it off with a flower crown and she was the most adorable ballerina. It's easy to make skirts and capes, which bring a lot to any costume.
- **Wear your PJs.** When we went to Target recently, we noticed that in the pajama department, there were all sorts of one-piece PJs that were different types of animals in both the children and adult

section. They were less than $20 and came with an attached hood to complete the look. The good thing about this is that you can wear them as regular PJs throughout the year—no one-hit wonders for *you*!

- **Paint faces.** You don't even have to buy actual face paint. Tap in to your inner makeup artist and watch some YouTube videos. You probably have everything you need to turn someone into a mermaid or another mythical creature.

Whatever you choose, be creative and you will find that you're completely original. After Halloween, relegate the costumes to the dress-up box so that your kids can enjoy them year-round. I used to always pick up leftover costumes the day after Halloween for even more dress-up fun.

*Candy*
Gone are the days when we could make delicious homemade treats to hand out. (At least in most neighborhoods.)

- **Buy candy *four* days before Halloween.** According to research by marketing specialists, that is the cheapest day pre-Halloween to make your purchase.
- **Buy in bulk.** The bigger the bag, the cheaper the stuff inside the bag is going to be.
- **Go off-brand.** Instead of buying from Hershey or Nestlé, consider buying something that isn't name brand.
- **Order non-food treats online**. You can visit a site like Oriental Trading Company to buy large bags of novelty toys. One of their bags will probably be enough little goodies to last you for a couple of years. Parents who have children with allergies will be really grateful, too.

*Decorations*
You don't have to spend $150 to have a super-spooky house!

- **Keep your decorations.** Keeping your decorations from year to year gives you a lot more oomph after you've been at it for a while. We've had a Halloween witch collection that I started when my oldest girl was two and added to for twenty years now.

- **Use things that aren't official Halloween decorations.** Do you have some fun antiques or other collections you could use for Halloween? We have things like old books, dingy antique bottles, candelabras, and decorative ceramic skulls that have a place in our normal décor. Not so spooky when they're spread out, but if you put them all together and add some dollar store black roses, you've got a Halloween display for your mantel.
- **Go to the dollar store.** You can get so many great things there for short-term decorations. Window clings, cheapo plastic tabletop decorations, and garland for a mere dollar! Don't forget the outdoor "spiderwebs" and spiders, and remember to add some old-school streamer garland.

*Pinterest and YouTube*

As with just about anything DIY, Pinterest and YouTube are the very best resources to find great ideas for a frugal Halloween. One day, I'm going to start a website called "Everything I Ever Needed to Know I Learned on YouTube." Dot-com, of course.

## A Thrifty Thanksgiving Feast from the Pantry

The holidays are wonderful, but they sure can be expensive. Many people don't want to spend a month's grocery budget on just one meal. Other families are having a tough time financially, either because of a job loss, a foreclosure, or exorbitant looming bills. When that's the case, the holidays can be a time for stress instead of enjoyment. Contrary to what you may think, you don't have to sell a kidney on the black market to put together a memorable and delicious Thanksgiving dinner. You can make a lot of it right from your pantry, and from reasonably priced items at the store.

If you've been building a stockpile, then the food in your pantry contains all sorts of basics for scratch cooking, purchased at the lowest prices available. Because of this, you can focus on purchasing only a few special items, like a turkey or a must-have goodie that is a tradition in your family, while you enjoy delicious yet thrifty treats for the rest of your Thanksgiving dinner. Break out the vintage cookbooks when looking for creative ways to use your pantry stockpile. My favorite cookbook is my old Fannie Farmer, which was written in 1896 and updated in the early 1900s. With these types of recipes, you won't be scurrying around looking for some of those crazy Martha

Stewart-esque gourmet ingredients like the breath of a yellow garden snail, captured during the second full moon of the month.

Make the presentation lovely, with fancy toothpicks in the appetizers, colorful napkins, and your nicest china. Use some of the fall décor ideas on page 201 for a festive table. If served with the proper flair—think candles, cloth napkins, and a beautiful presentation—any dinner seems just a little more festive. The following are some ideas for a festive meal that will make your guests feel well-fed and pampered, without emptying your pockets. You'll discover that many of the ingredients already reside in your pantry or are standard groceries that you'll have on hand, like eggs and cheese.

*Thrifty Appetizers and Party Snacks*
- Crackers (usually on sale during the holidays)
- Warm up a fruity jam, add some hot pepper flakes, and serve this over cream cheese for a deceptively elegant appetizer
- Homemade yogurt mixed with herbs to make a dip for veggies
- Breadsticks with marinara sauce
- Chex mix made with melted white chocolate
- Deviled eggs
- Garlic-roasted pumpkin seeds
- Make hummus from canned chickpeas
- Soup
- Slice a baguette, toast the slices, and serve with dishes of high-quality olive oil for dipping.

*Festive Platters*
Platters of cheeses and meats are pretty expensive choices. Simply removing things from jars and arranging them on a platter will make them look far more elegant than their humble origins.

- Place a variety of pickles on a dish for a relish tray.
- Olives and marinated vegetables create a lovely yet inexpensive antipasto.
- Don't buy the readymade veggie tray from the grocery store. Instead, peel and slice your carrots and cut up other veggies that you can find at a reasonable price.
- Instead of a fruit tray with out-of-season luxuries, go with fruits that are well-priced at this time of year, like mandarin oranges, pears, apples, and grapes.

*Thanksgiving Dinner Ideas*

Don't feel obligated to invest in out-of-season delicacies like fresh berries and asparagus in November. Splurge on a turkey and let the side dishes take a back seat. And if you can't afford the fanciest of dinners this year, don't despair. Roast a chicken instead of a turkey or a ham, or make some homemade stuffing baked with drumsticks. Things like stuffing (or dressing, depending on what part of the country you hail from) were originally created as a way to use up something that would ordinarily be thrown out: stale bread.

Channel your Depression-era ancestors and make your goodies the frugal, old-fashioned way.

- Homemade rolls or biscuits
- Pasta or potato salad
- Whip butter with a touch of honey—it makes the butter go further and looks fancy
- Canned or frozen veggies will seem more festive when topped with breadcrumbs, bacon, and/or cheese
- Mashed potatoes
- Scalloped potatoes
- Dumplings (maybe this is a Southern thing, but we always had dumplings with turkey dinner when I was a kid)
- Stuffing—save up your bread scraps or make a batch of homemade corn bread for the base
- Mashed sweet potatoes or winter squash with a sprinkle of brown sugar
- Homemade cranberry sauce (far tastier and about the same price as canned)

*Desserts*

Don't go all out on a bakery-made dessert. Make it from scratch from basic ingredients. Consider these humble ideas.

- Decorate a cake (or cupcakes) with fall-colored sprinkles
- Pies can be more expensive if you make the crust with pounds and pounds of butter. Try a single-crust pie or make it with shortening.
- Banana bread or pumpkin bread
- Homemade cookies
- Fruit crisp

- Pudding with whipped cream
- Brownies
- Ice cream (put it in cones or add some toppings to jazz things up)

**The most important ingredient.**
Remember, Thanksgiving is a tradition based on gratitude for a good harvest. We have so many things to be thankful for in this country, even when times are tough. The most important element of your Thanksgiving dinner isn't on the table—it's the people sitting around your table.

## Creating a Christmas Budget—and *Sticking to It*
There are two things that make all the difference in the world during the holidays. These two things mean the difference between starting the new year burdened with debt and starting it out free and clear.

1. Making a budget
2. Sticking to it

It sounds a lot easier than it actually is.

**How much can you really afford to spend?**
The first thing you need to do when setting a holiday budget is to take a cold hard look at reality. If you were not putting a single dime on a credit card, how much could you afford to spend on Christmas without having to shuffle around your other bills? For some of us, that amount may not be very high. I had a year once when all I could scrape together for gifts and food was an extra $100. That was the budget for me and two children. I didn't have credit cards or access to any other money. That was it.

And you know what? We had a great Christmas. We engulfed ourselves in traditions, made everything from scratch, hit the thrift stores, and upcycled. As worried as I was that my kids would feel let down, they weren't at all. They were thrilled with their modest gifts and enjoyed unwrapping them just as much as they would have enjoyed more expensive items. So, when you think about what you can afford, be realistic this year and *only* spend that.

**Figure out how that amount will break down.**
Once you know how much you're spending, make a list of the people for whom you need to get presents. During the Christmas I mentioned above, I

broke the budget down to $40 per girl, $10 for mom (so the kids could give me a present, too), and $10 for some treats to go with our holiday dinner. Because we didn't have a lot of extended family to buy for, it was a lot easier. We made cookies for neighbors, coworkers, and teachers from pantry supplies and everyone seemed delighted with our gifts. With your budget, do the same. How much will you spend per kid? Per adult? What will you do for friends, neighbors, and teachers? What about extended family?

**Sort out what you're spending ahead of time.**
I'm a big fan of the "envelope" method. Each year, I divvy up the cash into an envelope with a label on it: Kid 1, Kid 2, Christmas dinner, cookie supplies, charity, teachers—you get the idea.

This year, because I wanted to do some online shopping on Black Friday and Cyber Monday, I took the envelope method a step further and got prepaid Visas for part of the budget for each daughter. That way, I could still keep track of what I spent and keep things even. This allowed me to take advantage of some great online deals for desired items but didn't open up the whole of my bank balance to what I might spend on a whim.

**Let people know what to expect.**
The best way to head Christmas morning blues off at the pass is to make sure that everybody knows what to expect that year. Since my kids were old enough to understand it, I have always told them what their budgets were going to be. That way, they could make their wish lists accordingly. Also, by giving them these guidelines (and sticking to them) I taught them the very valuable lesson of . . . well, reality. Kids whose families put it all on plastic have no idea how much this stuff really costs in comparison to what Mom and Dad earn. How can we expect to raise kids who will be money-savvy adults if we shield them from financial realities?

Don't stop with your kids. If you have extended family that spends a fortune at the holidays, let them know that you will be doing things differently this year, perhaps with handmade gifts or something simple. Maybe other family members will also be on board with more simplicity—and perhaps they'll even be relieved.

**Stick to your budget.**
Once it's time to shop, it's essential that you stick to your budget. Put your envelopes in your purse and head out. When you get to the register, separate

your items into orders for different recipients. This way, you can pull cash from their envelope and stay organized by placing the receipt in that person's envelope. Don't worry about annoying the cashiers by splitting your purchases up. Be as swift and organized as you can but stick to your guns because this is the only way you will know when you have spent everything in your budget.

If there is money left over after your shopping trip, consider assigning it to a different envelope. You could splurge on an extra treat for your holiday mail or you could pop it into the charity envelope to help a family who is less fortunate.

**Stay organized.**
When you are finished shopping, keep your receipts in the appropriate envelope. This will make your life much easier if something needs to be returned after Christmas.

**Stop spending!**
One issue that I sometimes have when I get all my holiday shopping done early is that I am tempted to keep spending. If something "perfect" catches my eye after my shopping is complete, it can be hard to say no to it. Then, especially if it is something for one of my children, I feel obligated to get something for my other daughter. And round and round it goes.

I avoid this by staying out of the stores once I am finished shopping. Retailers pay marketers bundles of money to help part you with yours and they have all sorts of sneaky strategies. We'll talk about that next.

**The traps retailers use to get you to exceed your Christmas budget (and how to avoid them).**
As adults, we've all discovered the painful truth that it isn't Santa Claus paying for the big stack of ever-more-expensive presents under the Christmas tree. It's us, and we've learned the hard way that it's not just the "most wonderful time of the year." It's the most expensive time of the year.

Not only do we have to strive to keep up with our family's expectations, but we are also the targets of retailers who are doing everything they can to get you to exceed your Christmas budget and spend more than ever. They're backing up their efforts with science, using surveys and psychological strategies to manipulate customers for more profit.

**Most people spent more last year than the year before.**
In 2019, spending in the US increased by 3.6 percent, to $655.8 billion. Let's break this down on a more individual level, because when I read about billions of dollars, I tend to zone out. According to a survey done by The American Research Group, most Americans planned to increase holiday gift-giving expenditures by an average of 5% to $929.[1]

But there are other criteria that relate to average spending. The survey also found:

- The average spending for those saying they plan to make catalog purchases is $1,225.
- The average planned spending by those saying they will make purchases on the Internet is $1,342.
- Shoppers saying they will pay full price (instead of waiting for sales) plan on spending $1,212.
- Those waiting for sales plan on spending $834.
- The average planned spending for shoppers who have already started their holiday shopping is $1,182.
- The average for those who have not started their shopping is $765.

So, if we were to base our budget and timing on this survey, the way to spend the least is to shop in person, look for sales, and hold off on shopping instead of getting an early start.

**Retailers are going to do their best to get you to spend more.**
Smart retailers are reading the statistics above, too. Especially in brick-and-mortar stores, where sales are down slightly, they'll be pulling out all the stops to get you to exceed your budget. According to an article from the National Retail Foundation,[2] "Holiday budgets are set in pencil, not stone."

A survey conducted to see how people could be persuaded to part with more money than they had originally planned on spending found that

---

1   Amanda C. Haury, "Average Cost of an American Christmas," Investopedia, Nov. 8, 2019, https://www.investopedia.com/financial-edge/1112/average-cost-of-an-american-christmas.aspx

2   Allison Zeller, "Holiday Budgets Are Set in Pencil, Not Stone," National Retail Federation, Nov. 9, 2016, https://nrf.com/blog/holiday-budgets-are-set-pencil-not-stone

customers were persuaded to spend anywhere from $25 to $200 beyond their original budgets. Below, you can see the top five reasons people parted with extra money and the percentage of people who said they'd be likely to do so.

- A really good sale or promotion: 51%
- Seeing the perfect gift for someone I didn't originally plan to buy for: 34%
- Finding something perfect for myself: 27%
- Free shipping with no minimum threshold: 27%
- Needing additional items for last-minute parties: 17%

The article also suggests that convenience, like easy returns and delivery, can make people more likely to spend, particularly people over the age of sixty-five. And finally, expert salespeople can persuade people to purchase more expensive versions of items they are seeking, or even things that were never on the shopping list to begin with.

The NRF concludes, "Shoppers can be convinced to spend more than they originally budgeted for but may need a little convincing or inspiration. Retailers can try these tactics to earn more of those spontaneous sales."

**The most important things you can do are to make a Christmas budget and stick to it.**

As you can see, retailers and marketers strategize all year long to figure out how to part you from your money. If you are aiming for a simpler holiday season, having financial difficulties this year, or just want to be able to face the New Year without holiday debt looming over your head, it's essential that you understand the ways they're trying to manipulate you.

## Setting a Frugal & Festive Holiday Table

Photos abound this time of year with beautifully set holiday tables. How can you possibly compete when you're on a budget? There are all sorts of things you can do that will make your tablescape stand out, often without spending any extra money.

*Dishes*

Contrary to what sellers would have you believe, you don't need a separate set of dishes just for the holidays.

- **If you have fancy china, use it!** Maybe this is the Southern gal in me, but growing up we always had everyday china and fine china. As an adult, my own fine china comes from a yard sale, but lots of folks get fancy table settings as wedding gifts.
- **Use solid color dishes.** If your everyday dishes are simple, they can easily be dressed up for the holidays. Our everyday dishes are white. I have an assortment of different patterns and textures, but they are all white. I can use these with colorful tablecloths and centerpieces for a festive look.
- **Some folks use paper plates.** Some families don't worry about "fancy" and go with "practical." If this is you, check out your dollar store for festive holiday paper plates. Get more than you need, because people will use separate ones for different courses.

*Serving*

The way you serve your food can make it look much more festive.

- **Transfer everything into nice serving dishes for a table that looks more elegant.** Whether your food is store-bought or homemade, it will look better in a serving dish than the container from the store or the pot you cooked it in.
- **Pick up serving dishes throughout the year.** This may not help you right now, but for future reference, look for attractive serving dishes when you hit yard sales and thrift stores. Because of my white color scheme, my additions always blend nicely. You may be able to find a few pieces at the thrift store or dollar store if you're in a pinch right now.
- **Pick up serving utensils on a dime.** If you don't have serving utensils, they can often be found at thrift stores and dollar stores. If they're plain or unattractive, you can temporarily jazz them up by wrapping the handles in twine. Clearly, this must be removed before washing. I pick up vintage silver-plate utensils every time I see them at a good price.
- **Fancy toothpicks and flags make things festive.** For a cute display of appetizers, pop some of those fancy toothpicks in each item. The baking aisle of your local craft store will also have little flag-topped toothpicks designed for cupcakes for even more holiday flair. I've also found these at the dollar store.

*Linens and Décor*

These extra touches can produce a lovely table that everyone will admire.

- **Use a tablecloth.** For the adult table, a beautiful table cloth is the perfect base for your meal. The cloth doesn't have to be Christmas-y to work. If it's the right size, even a pretty sheet or curtain panel could work. Again, if you don't have this, the thrift store is your friend.
- **The napkins can be cloth or festive paper holiday napkins.** We buy plain, colorful paper napkins any time we see them at a good price, as well as post-holiday festive napkins.
- **Napkin rings don't have to be $18 from the import store.** You can use twine, yarn, or get the kids involved in decorating rings made from adult-cut toilet paper rolls.
- **Centerpieces need not be store-bought.** Do you have old ornaments missing their hanging loops? Place them in clear vases or bowls on the table. Intersperse candles (non-scented) and fresh greenery from the nearest evergreen tree down the center of the table. Found objects that go along with your theme (like seashells, river stones, or pine cones) can be added to the display.

Of course, the most important things of beauty around a Christmas table are the faces of the people you love.

## The Frugalite Holiday Gift Guide

Whether they'll admit it or not, everyone loves getting presents, and during the holidays, we love *giving* them too. (Although the thing I personally hate is being forced into a gift exchange with folks I don't know.) That little moment of grinchiness aside, you can really break the budget with gifts. Here are a few ideas that may help you tap into your inner Frugalite.

*Kits*

We like giving "kits" as presents. If they're presented festively, an inexpensive kit can be a welcome gift. Here are some ideas we have used over the years. Wrap them in cellophane, top them with a jaunty bow, and add a gift card.

- **Pasta dinner kit:** Layer a colander with festive shredded paper. Arrange a box of spaghetti noodles, a jar of nice-quality (or better yet, homemade) marinara sauce, a triangle of fresh Parmesan with a mini grater, some crushed chili peppers, Italian seasoning, and a pasta spoon.

- **Bath kit:** Use a basket as the base—I pick up baskets for a quarter at the local thrift store. Add in homemade or store-bought bath products, one of those microfiber hair wraps (available at the dollar store), some folded washcloths or a loofah, and a handful of sea shells (also available at the dollar store). Top it off with a back scrubber.
- **Game kit:** Head to the dollar store and pick up an assortment of brainteaser games, à la Cracker Barrel. Look for those triangle peg games, Rubik's cubes, Chinese checkers, and a wooden tic-tac-toe set. Pop them into a sturdy tote bag tied with a festive bow.
- **Ice cream sundae kit:** Find a cute basket and fill it with everything but the ice cream—waffle cone cups, toppings, sprinkles, and jars of caramel and fudge sauce.
- **Night at the movies kit:** Put everything in a large popcorn bowl. Fill it with bags of popcorn kernels (you can fill goodie bags and tie them with twine), popcorn seasoning, 3D glasses (available at the dollar store), a can of soda for each family member, and an assortment of candy.

### Gifts in Jars

Don't think you have to do an ornate basket if money is tight. Gifts in jars can also be creative yet thrifty. You can layer all manner of things in jars for a charming, homespun gift. As a bonus, if you have a well-stocked pantry, you may already have the supplies on hand.

Here are a few ideas. Simply layer the ingredients in the jar.

- Bean soup
- Cookie mix
- Chocolate chip pancake mix
- Hot cocoa mix
- Chai tea
- Muffin mix

The sky's the limit. Don't forget the instructions! Handwrite them or print them out on attractive paper to include with the jar. Be creative and consider the kinds of things the recipient likes. You can't go wrong with something from the heart.

# *Conclusion*

I have three wishes for this book.

First, if you are struggling and you happen upon this guide, we may not know each other personally but I feel kinship with you because I have been where you are right now. I hope that the information within this book helps you through this difficult period and reminds you that there is a beautiful light at the end of what feels right now like a dark endless tunnel. I've been there. It's awful. It isn't your fault, and even if it is because you made some mistakes, this doesn't define you. It won't be like this forever, my friend.

Second, if you have dreams that have always felt out of reach, I hope my book can help you see the glorious possibilities. I want you to live comfortably. I want you to know that you can travel. You can help your family members. You can pay off your debts. You can live a life that is not a constant financial struggle. It's all within your reach.

And finally, my hope for you is that this book helps light your imagination on fire. Frugality doesn't have to be torture—and if you expect to stick to it for long, it shouldn't be. My frugal journey has helped me do many things:

- Put my children through college debt-free
- Start my own business
- Travel extensively
- Live comfortably with less stress

And even better, it's helped me to focus on the things—and most importantly, the people—who are truly essential. By focusing my money and my efforts, I have been fortunate enough to have incredible experiences. I've made memories. I've spent time with my beloved girls and built relationships with them that other people comment on in wonder.

You don't have to do exotic things, either. You can make precious memories just walking down the road together. In the end, nobody remembers fondly that you spent $5,000 on that one meal or that you had four cars in the driveway. The people who truly love you don't care about that stuff. They remember the time you spent together, the experiences they had with you, and that you made them feel treasured and important.

The real gift of frugality is not just seeing the price of things. It's seeing the things that are priceless.

# Appendix
## In Season and On Sale

If you know the sales cycles used by the retail industry, you can save a *lot* of money. Seasonal produce will also save you a fortune on healthy fruits and vegetables.

## January

### In Season:
- Bananas
- Beets
- Broccoli
- Brussels sprouts
- Cabbage
- Carrots
- Cauliflower
- Celeriac
- Grapefruit
- Kale
- Leeks
- Lemons
- Mushrooms
- Onions
- Oranges
- Parsnips
- Pears
- Potatoes
- Rutabagas
- Sweet potatoes
- Turnips
- Winter squash

### On Sale:
- Calendars
- Holiday gift wrap and decorations
- Holiday candy
- Video games
- Perfume/fragrances
- Electronics
- Furniture
- Fitness supplies and equipment
- Clothing
- Flooring

## February

Wondering what things are on sale and in season this month? Here are your lists to help you shop for the best deals of February!

**In Season:**
- Bananas
- Cabbage
- Grapefruit
- Leeks
- Lemons
- Mushrooms
- Onions
- Oranges
- Pears
- Potatoes
- Rutabagas
- Sweet potatoes and yams
- Tangerines
- Turnips
- Winter squash

**On Sale:**
- Bicycles
- Canned food
- Cell phones
- Chocolate (after Valentine's Day)
- Indoor fitness equipment
- Outdoor furniture (retailers want you shopping for spring ASAP since all the winter holidays are over)
- Perfume/cologne (post-Valentine)
- Secondhand fitness equipment (from those resolutions that never came to fruition)
- Super Bowl party supplies
- TVs

We'll be having some cabbage dishes, some potato and leek soup, and some delicious roasted veggies this month. It's good that citrus is in season right now, because it's the ideal time to increase your vitamin C with all of these nasty viruses going around.

## March

Ahhh . . . March. This is the time that you may actually begin to find fresh local produce, depending on your climate. I'll be starting some spinach, radishes, and snow peas in my own garden. Here are the produce items that are in-season right now:

**In Season:**
- Asparagus
- Bananas
- Broccoli
- Cabbage
- Lettuce
- Mangos
- Mushrooms
- Onions and leeks
- Peas
- Pineapple
- Rhubarb

- Spinach
- Strawberries

**On Sale:**
- Frozen food
- Spring cleaning supplies
- Easter food (ham, candy)
- Digital cameras
- Humidifiers

- Small consumer electronics (MP3, DVD, and Blu-ray, etc.)
- TVs
- Winter coats, gloves, hats, scarves (last-chance sales)
- Cookware
- Luggage
- Kitchen accessories
- Vacuums

This is also the perfect time to hit the thrift stores and take advantage of other people's spring-cleaning frenzies!

## April

If you're buying, these are the things to look for in April.

**In Season:**
- Apricots
- Asparagus
- Bananas
- Beets
- Broccoli
- Cabbage
- Green beans
- Lettuce
- Mangos
- Mushrooms
- Onions and leeks
- Peas
- Pineapple

- Radishes
- Rhubarb
- Spinach
- Strawberries

**On Sale:**
- Outdoor fitness gear
- Running/walking shoes
- Easter décor
- Candy
- Spring décor
- Jewelry
- Cruises

## May

Buying fresh foods that are in-season will save you a fortune on your grocery bill. Here are the things to look for in May.

**In Season:**
- Asparagus
- Bananas

- Beets
- Garlic
- Green beans

- Lettuce
- Mangos
- Mushrooms
- Onions and leeks
- Peas
- Pineapple
- Radishes
- Rhubarb
- Small baby potatoes
- Spinach
- Strawberries

**On Sale:**
- Refrigerators
- Mattresses
- Office furniture
- Mexican food (Cinco de Mayo)
- Grilling food and supplies
- Gym memberships
- Spring clearance clothing

## June

**In Season:**
- Apricots
- Bell peppers
- Blackberries
- Blueberries
- Cantaloupe
- Cherries
- Corn
- Cucumbers
- Eggplant
- Garlic
- Grapes
- Green beans
- Honeydew melon
- Lima beans
- Peaches
- Peas

- Plums
- Raspberries
- Summer squash and zucchini
- Tomatoes
- Watermelon

**On Sale:**
- Gym memberships
- Tools
- "Guy" stuff (Father's Day)
- Picnic items
- Grills and related accessories
- Sunscreen
- Hair removal products
- Bug spray
- Swimsuits
- Flip flops

## July

This is one of the best times of year to get delicious things in season. Here's the list—and it's *huge*! Consider grabbing extra of some of your favorites and preserving it by freezing, canning, or turning it into jam for times of the year when it isn't so inexpensive.

**In Season:**
- Apricots
- Bananas
- Basil
- Beets
- Bell peppers
- Blackberries
- Blueberries
- Cantaloupe
- Cherries
- Corn
- Cucumbers
- Eggplant
- Garlic
- Grapefruit
- Grapes
- Green beans
- Honeydew melon
- Kiwifruit
- Lima beans
- Mushrooms
- Peaches
- Peas
- Plums
- Radishes
- Raspberries
- Strawberries
- Summer squash and zucchini
- Tomatoes
- Watermelon

**On Sale:**
- School supplies
- Canning supplies
- Laptops
- Summer clothes and shoes

This is a great time of year to get certain things on sale. Although the season is in full force, to retailers it's beginning to wrap up, so you can find great deals on all things summer. As well, some retailers will start their back-to-school sales early, so be on the lookout for killer deals.

## August

What should you shop for this month? Typically, anything related to back-to-school will be on sale, as will items that pertain to summer. Watch for tax-free days in your state to save another 5 to 15 percent in sales tax.

**In Season:**
- Apricots
- Beets
- Bell peppers
- Blackberries
- Blueberries
- Cantaloupe
- Cherries
- Corn
- Cucumbers
- Eggplant
- Garlic
- Grapefruit
- Grapes
- Green beans
- Honeydew melon
- Kiwifruit
- Lima beans

- Mushrooms
- Peaches
- Peas
- Plums
- Radishes
- Raspberries
- Strawberries
- Summer squash and zucchini
- Tomatoes
- Watermelon

**On Sale:**
- Bedding
- Organizers
- Kids' clothes
- School supplies
- Summer clothing
- Swimsuits
- Sunscreen
- Bug repellant
- Outdoor furniture
- Barbecues and barbecue accessories

## September

**In Season:**
- Apples
- Broccoli
- Brussel sprouts
- Cabbage
- Cauliflower
- Celery root
- Cranberries (grab them now and freeze enough for the holidays)
- Cucumbers
- Dates
- Fennel
- Grapes
- Greens
- Iceberg lettuce
- Leaf lettuce
- Mushrooms
- Nuts
- Okra
- Tomatoes

**On Sale:**
- Old generation iPhones (The new ones are coming soon—the price will drop by at least 50% on the old ones!)
- School snacks like pudding cups, juice boxes, etc.
- Car accessories
- Cars (they're making room for the new model year)
- Furniture
- Mattresses
- Appliances
- Barbecues
- Bicycles
- Garden supplies
- Lawnmowers and landscaping tools
- Patio furniture
- Summer clothes
- Swimsuits

If there are some bigger items you need, September may be the month! Watch for Labor Day weekend sales, too. This can be the cheapest time of the year to buy certain high-ticket items. And don't forget the end of summer sales!

## October

- **In Season:**
- Apples
- Bananas
- Beets
- Broccoli
- Brussels sprouts
- Carrots
- Cauliflower
- Cranberries
- Garlic
- Ginger
- Grapes
- Mushrooms
- Parsnips
- Pears
- Pineapple
- Pumpkins
- Sweet potatoes and yams
- Winter squash

**On Sale:**
- Barbecues
- Grilling supplies
- Air conditioners
- Fans
- Plants
- Seeds
- Outdoor furniture
- Jeans

## November

**In Season:**
- Apples
- Bananas
- Beets
- Broccoli
- Brussels sprouts
- Carrots
- Cauliflower
- Cranberries
- Garlic
- Ginger
- Grapes
- Mushrooms
- Parsnips
- Pears
- Pineapple
- Pumpkins
- Sweet potatoes and yams
- Winter squash

**On Sale:**
- Halloween candy
- String lights
- Decorations
- Costumes
- Baking items: baking powder, baking soda, cornmeal, flour, white sugar, brown sugar, powdered sugar, Bisquick, cake/brownie/cookie mixes, canned frostings
- Peanut butter
- Holiday foods: gravy, gravy mixes, seasoning packets, broth, Stove Top stuffing, corn bread mixes, canned dried onions, canned pumpkin
- Turkey
- Black Friday deals

## December

Below, you'll find a list of items that are traditionally great buys in the month of December. Not only are there some awesome post-Christmas sales (which we talked about in detail already), but other items are frequently reduced this month.

**In Season:**
- Bananas
- Grapefruit
- Lemons
- Oranges
- Pears
- Mushrooms
- Onions
- Leeks
- Potatoes
- Rutabagas
- Sweet Potatoes/yams
- Parsnips
- Turnips
- Winter squash
-
- **On Sale:**
- Cookies
- Crackers
- Dips
- Sour cream
- Butter
- Cold cuts
- Soft drinks
- Stuffing mix
- Potato mix
- Corn bread mix
- Potatoes
- **Candy-making items:** chocolate chips, sprinkles, vanilla, corn syrup, nuts, evaporated milk, marshmallows

- **Baking items:** Baking powder, baking soda, cornmeal, flour, white sugar, brown sugar, powdered sugar, Bisquick, cake/brownie/cookie mixes, canned frostings, pie crusts
- **Holiday foods:** gravy, gravy mixes, seasoning packets, broth, canned dried onions, cranberry and canned pumpkin, ham
- Frozen potatoes, pies, whipped topping, vegetables
- Champagne
- Golf clubs
- Pools
- Televisions and other electronics (only before Christmas—afterward the prices go back up)
- Tools
- Fall-themed décor
- Gift cards—these are often a promotion at the checkout counter of your favorite stores (I have gotten gift cards that are reduced by as much as 10 to 15 percent—and you don't have to give them as gifts! If you know it is a place you normally shop, you can keep them for discounted shopping in the future.)

# About the Author

Daisy Luther is a coffee-swigging, globe-trotting blogger who writes about current events, emergency preparedness, frugality, and the pursuit of liberty on her website, TheOrganicPrepper.com. She writes about living large on a small budget on another of her websites, TheFrugalite.com, and she writes about her travels on DaisyLuther.com.

Daisy is the author of five books and runs a small digital publishing company that focuses on preparedness, frugality, and survival.

# Acknowledgments

This book wouldn't be possible without the following people:

**My girls:** You two were the inspiration for it all. Like, I kind of want to pull out the embarrassing baby pictures so show everyone how fabulous you've always been. Y'all kept me accountable for our financial goals and were so loving and tolerant of my wacky money-saving experiments. I'm *so* proud when I see you out there cheapin' it up in your own homes now. Rock. Stars.

**My besties:** OMG. You guys. What would I do without the insomnia chats, the crazy adventures, the lunches, the unconditional friendship, and the get-your-butt-in-gear tough love when I need it? I am so fortunate to have you bad-ass, kick-ass, cool-ass people in my corner. You are my lifeboats in a wild and stormy sea. You have always, always been there for me. You are my chosen family.

# Index